MIND TAVERN

MIND TAVERN

Essential Music Playlists for the Headphone Generation

STARK HUNTER

Copyright 2024 by Stark Hunter

Paperback ISBN: 978-1-63337-774-5
E-Book ISBN: 978-1-63337-775-2
LCCN: 2024902260

Published by Mind Tavern Books
Book Design and Production by Columbus Publishing Lab
www.columbuspublishinglab.com

All rights reserved. No part of this book may be reproduced or transmitted in any form or by any means, electronic or mechanical, including photocopying, recording, or by any information storage and retrieval system, without permission in writing from the copyright owners.

Photographs from the Stark Hunter Collection.

TABLE OF CONTENTS

Introduction I	. . . .	i
Introduction II	Primary Musical Influences from Childhood and Teenage Years	v
Playlist #1	'The Guitar Hero".	1
Playlist #2	The Saxophone and the Human Voice" . . .	7
Playlist #3	"The Best in 'Live' Music".	13
Playlist #4	"Best All-Time Album — Abbey Road". .	19
Playlist #5	"Musical Obsessions"	25
Playlist #6	"Musical Pieces I Have Enjoyed Down Through The Years"	31
Playlist #7	"Classic Country, Mahler and Stravinsky".	37
Playlist #8	"Cocktails for the Soul" Post War Jazz of the 1950's	43
Playlist #9	"Best of 1970"	49
Playlist #10	"My Best Emotional Friends in 2005" . .	55
Playlist #11	"Video Musical Masterpieces".	61
Playlist #12	"Music for Solo Piano and New York, New York!"	65
Playlist #13	"Play These Before You Die"	71
Playlist #14	"We Are The Music Makers; We Are The Dreamers Of Dreams"	75
Playlist #15	"Brian Eno (and two friends)".	79
Playlist #16	"23 of My Favorite 45's from the 1950's" .	83

Playlist #17	"Wendy's List and Personal Favorites from the Past"	91
Playlist #18	"Live Video Performances from Ed Sullivan, Woodstock and the Fillmore"	97
Playlist #19	"Music I've Been Listening to Lately"	103
Playlist #20	"A Trip To Lovell's Record Store"	107
Playlist #21	"Igor Stravinsky and The Rite Of Spring"	113
Playlist #22	"The Greatest Rock And Roll Band Of All Time"	117
Playlist #23	"The Moody Blues" The Best of 1967 – 1972	121
Playlist #24	"Salute To The Jimi Hendrix Experience"	127
Playlist #25	"The 1960's – Decade of Transcendence"	133
Playlist #26	"A You Tube Experience"	141
Playlist #27	"20 Compelling 'Headphone' Albums"	145
Addenda		155
Index		163
About the Author		175

"Music hath charms to soothe a savage breast. To soften rocks, or bend the knotted oak."

— William Congreve (1670-1729)

INTRODUCTION
I

THIS BOOK IS ABOUT the best 'Headphone Music' ever recorded.

Well, at least in the opinion of this California writer, a baby boomer and old hippie, born in 1952— this is the best music to hear while wearing headphones, or in today's vernacular, ear buds. It consists of 27 recommended "headphone" playlists, written from 2001 to 2014. I spent 13 years reading and researching articles on music history, plus spending hundreds of hours exploring and listening to recommended albums, cassettes and 8-Track tapes—mostly from a half century ago.

My listening 'Odyssey' was not done in solitude, however. One 'old hippy' friend of mine was on board with me, Dennis F, and was privy to my carefully chosen pieces, and likewise listened with open, unbiased ears and a curious heart during all those years. It is hoped the readers of this book will approach these lists with the same equanimity. It is also recommended that the reader actually makes the effort to look up these carefully chosen recommendations, and spend quality time listening to them, preferably with headphones or ear buds on. That is the point of this book.

Truth be known: It is a far different (and more satisfying) listening experience when no one else can hear what you are hearing—that is, wonderful musical sounds in the privacy of your own ears, and mind. There is an indescribable intimacy involved when it is just you, the listener, and the music. Thank goodness for headphones—they provide the Cone of Silence, wherein listeners can escape to their own private worlds of music and sound.

Incidentally, most, if not all, of the musical titles mentioned in this book can be found and heard online at Youtube, Spotify and Amazon Music.

It goes without saying that I am surely not a professional musicologist, or a recognized expert on these matters. I am just an old hippie record fan from the Boomer Generation who has been intently listening to music since 1955— all genres of music; Jazz, Big Band, Rock and Roll, Blues, Motown, Pop, Classical, Ethnic, Movie Soundtracks, and Miscellaneous.

Though I have no credentials to do so, I still offer up these homespun suggestions for what I personally consider to be the apex of Twentieth Century "Headphone Music." This was all gleaned together after 67 years of personal listening, and it is realized that many people would disagree with some of these musical inclusions. And that is fine. These are my lists. Publish your own lists if you are so inclined.

As the reader peruses my lists, certain obscure references are mentioned— namely, the bands to which I was associated back in the 70's. Included also are the names of old personal friends who are connected to the music in memory only. Their surnames are not fully revealed but initialed.

Welcome to Mind Tavern

Stark Hunter
2024

Pictured here are listeners Stark Hunter and Dennis F in 1972

INTRODUCTION II

Primary Musical Influences from Childhood and Teenage Years

MY EARLIEST MEMORIES as a youth growing up in Whittier California during the 50's and 60's consisted of spending countless hours playing records on the family hi-fi system and listening to radio stations KFWB and KRLA. The first popular song I became endeared to was "Green Door" by Jim Lowe. I was a four year old living in a duplex, and I played that piece over and over incessantly, no doubt driving my parents crazy. "Dark Moon" by Gale Storm also had an impact on me as a child. Her rich alto voice sent shivers down my young spine. When Elvis Presley recorded "Hound Dog," it was a sensation. I vividly recall winning a coin toss with my brother over who would get to buy that particular 45.

As the 50's merged into the 60's, my 45 record collection expanded, and included the likes of the Big Bopper, Chubby Checker, Ricky Nelson, Richie Valens, Buddy Holly, and later, the Beach Boys and the Beatles. Songs that I literally played to death were "Hard Headed Woman" by Elvis, "Searchin" by the Coasters, "The Twist" by Chubby Checker, "Surfing Bird" by the Trashmen, "Surfin' Safari" by the Beach Boys and "I Saw You Standing There" by the Beatles. These were the pieces that set the stage for my more serious musical interests of the late 60's, when I received my first stereo system on Christmas Day, 1968.

Like most music aficionados, I developed manias for different rock groups, and experienced nirvana in my bedroom, as my stereo record player boomed full blast, with repeated playings of the same music; each mania sometimes lasting 3 to 4 months. For awhile, I was obsessed with the "Sgt. Pepper " album by the Beatles. I was completely blown away by John Lennon's "A Day In The Life." Then it was "Magical Mystery Tour" with "Penny Lane," The Fool On The Hill" and "I Am The Walrus." And finally the "White Album," in my opinion, their masterpiece album, and even better than the esteemed "Sgt. Pepper." Most of my all-time favorite Beatle pieces appear on the White Album: "Blackbird," "Helter Skelter," "Martha My Dear," "Honey Pie," "Dear Prudence" and the fascinating "Revolution No. 9."

From there I got hooked on the rock poetry of The Doors. "Light My Fire," "The End" and "When The Music's Over" are, in my opinion, three of the greatest rock pieces in the history of Rock and Roll. It wasn't long before I heard about the psychedelic rock of the Jimi Hendrix Experience. "Foxy Lady" and "Purple Haze" were pieces so different, and so awesome in sound, I literally wore the record out to the point of complete inaudibility. No one could play the guitar like Hendrix, and obviously his music had a profound effect, not just on me, but on the entire "Boomer Nation" as well.

Cream was another group I admired, especially their two album set "Wheels Of Fire." I couldn't believe this album contained a ten minute drum solo by Ginger Baker on the song "Toad." Midway through the summer of 1969, my mania turned in the direction of the country rock sounds of Creedence Clearwater Revival. For a couple months, "Keep On Chooglin" was the only song that could be heard through the open window of my Hoover Street bedroom. Other bands that I played to death on my stereo were Grand Funk Railroad, Canned Heat, Savoy Brown, Led Zeppelin, Ten Years After, The Who, Crosby Stills Nash, Santana and Johnny Winter.

The albino guitarist, Johnny Winter, not only looked weird but he was the fastest guitarist I had ever heard. I remember writing a term paper on this guy while a senior in high school. Santana's "Black Magic Woman" was playing quietly on the stereo when I lost my virginity making love to my girlfriend in 1971.

"The Boogie" by Savoy Brown was my current mania when my girlfriend gave me her "kiss of death" in 1971. Grand Funk's "Paranoid" used to get me all hyper and spaced out when I turned it up full blast in my room. The same with Led Zeppelin; playing "Whole Lotta Love" and "Dazed and Confused" would leave me shaking like some spastic madman. Jimmy Page was the "High Priest" of rock guitar heroes of that time. He was smooth, fast, eclectic and a virtuoso.

Another guitar virtuoso was Alvin Lee of Ten Years After. I believe his performance on the film Woodstock had more of an impact on me than even Jimi Hendrix's version of the National Anthem, and that performance floored me. Lee's "I'm Going Home," in my opinion, is the top performance of the 1969 Woodstock Music Festival. I must've played that piece a thousand times on my stereo during the summer of 1970.

"Suite: Judy Blue Eyes" by Crosby Stills and Nash made a major impact on me. In fact, every cut on their first album is interesting and compelling listening. "Refried Boogie" by Canned Heat was another piece I became obsessed with. Their relentless driving boogie beat, and the high pitched vocals of Al "Blind Owl" Wilson, made this band one of my all-time favorites. My interest in "boogie" music next lead me to the Rolling Stones.

I was stoked when I first heard "Midnight Rambler" from their "Ya Ya's" album. I used to play that piece full blast over and over again in my office room on Hoover Street. Finally, "Live At Leeds," by the loudest (decibel-wise) band in the history of rock and roll, The Who, for at least a month, blasted down the hallway and through the shaded rooms of the Hoover Street home of my youth.

**MIND TAVERN
THE PLAYLISTS**

PLAYLIST #1
"THE GUITAR HERO"

I HAVE ALWAYS BEEN suitably impressed with guitar players; I suppose it goes back to the late 50's when I used to sneak into my brother's bedroom while he was out delivering newspapers and play his Chuck Berry 45's on his keen, auto-replay, "45" record player. To this day I still dig the rock n' roll twang of this legendary rock performer, and you'll notice that I begin and end this two day playlist with this archetype "Guitar Hero," the real "King of Rock n' Roll."

You may disagree with this subjective moniker, but if not the "King," then at least he is the "Father." From there, you will notice that I have placed subsequent "Guitar Heroes" in chronological order starting in the early 60's with the best of the "surf guitar," and ending with 90's "grunge… Kurt Cobain style."

You will also notice that most of the greatest "Guitar Heroes" are congregated around the peak years of 1969 to 1970, when "Guitar Hero" worship was at its most intense. There are so many inspiring guitar artists that I have heard and thoroughly enjoyed down through the years, so it was extremely difficult to narrow them down to two measly hours; and so here they are— names like Dick Dale, Eric Clapton, Stephen Stills, Jimi Hendrix, Jimmy Page, Robert Fripp, Alvin Lee, Frank Zappa, Jim McCarty, Johnny Winter, "Lonesome" Dave Peverette, Kim Simmonds, J.C. Fogerty, Dickie Betts, John Lennon, (of course—how can we have a "Guitar Hero" playlist without a Beatle?) and even a fellow named Jeff Floro, are included. Basically speaking, all of these guys had one distinct musical quality in common— they could "wail," "kick ass" or "rock out" on the electric guitar.

PLAYLIST (PART ONE)

1. Chuck Berry – "School Days" – (2:30) 1957
Definitely my favorite from the Great 28, recorded with Chess records. When I hear this, my mind instantly remembers back to the late 50's, fishing off the Newport pier with my dad and brother, baiting our hooks until 3 in the morning, listening to KFWB on a transistor radio; invariably it was Chuck Berry rocking and a reeling in the salty night air.

2. Dick Dale and his Del-Tones – "King of the Surf Guitar" (2:10) 1963
What can I say? If you grew up in southern California in the early 60's, then you knew of the King of the Surf Guitar himself—Dick Dale. Today it's all a bunch of nostalgic kitsch, but back in 1963, I dug his guitar music.

3. Dick Dale and his Del-Tones – "Hava Nagila" (2:03) 1963
One of the best surfing instrumentals of all time. Back in 1964 I would dance like a possessed kid to this song. My mother probably thought I needed a psychiatrist, or a Catholic priest, asap.

4. Stephen Stills and the Buffalo Springfield – "Bluebird" (4:28) 1967
The highlight of this seminal 60's classic is Stills' superb work on the acoustic guitar. A masterpiece.

5. Jimi Hendrix Experience – "Voodoo Chile" (Live Version from *Electric Ladyland*) 1968 (14:00)
Amazing virtuosity here. You can't get much better than this – Jimi

Hendrix having an outrageous jam session with his friends—Stevie Winwood being one of them on the organ. I can recall hearing this entire jam on KNAC – FM radio one late summer night in 1970, and I remember being simply astounded by it. Hendrix definitely ranks #1 in my book for pure technical craftsmanship as a rock guitarist.

6. Johnny Winter – "Hustled Down In Texas" from *Second Winter* 1968 (4:30)

I was so amazed by the technical mastery of Johnny Winter back in 1970 that I decided to do my 12th grade English term paper on this guitarist. This piece is a tightly played blues romp straight from the rock saloons of Texas, Winter's home state and cradle for his long rock career. He is definitely in my "Top 3" as "Greatest Guitar Hero."

7. Eric Clapton and Cream – "Crossroads" from *Wheels of Fire* 1968 (4:24)

The summer of 1969 was the summer I discovered Eric Clapton's sheer genius on electric guitar. This is perhaps his best recorded performance, although I'm sure there are others that are as equally amazing. Listen as he "cooks" with Jack Bruce on Bass and Ginger Baker on Drums. This is Cream's finest moment in concert, in my opinion.

8. Alvin Lee and Ten Years After – "I'm Going Home" *Woodstock*, 1969. (9:49)

I present this stand out moment from Woodstock – "Pretty face" Alvin Lee (as Rolling Stone magazine described him) and his back-up band, Ten Years After, rocking out in the wee hours of the morning. I chose this DVD clip because the image of this English rocker, peace sign on his Gibson guitar, playing fast and furious, epitomizes the classic "Guitar Hero" persona. Hearing one (a rock guitar virtuoso) is great, but seeing one in action is another thing entirely.

9. Frank Zappa – "Willie the Pimp," *Hot Rats* 1969 (9:25)

One of my favorite guitar effects back in 1970 was the wah-wah pedal. Zappa plays a mean rock guitar on this piece, utilizing skillfully this wah-wah device.

10. Kim Simmonds and Savoy Brown – "Savoy Brown Boogie," *A Step Further* (22:07) 1969

Kim Simmonds could "rock out" on guitar with the best of them. I say this with confidence because I saw and heard this guy in concert back in 1970 in Santa Monica. All those stoned rock n' roll fans there that night were dancing in the aisles and on their folding chairs as Simmonds played some of the best rock guitar I had ever heard.

PLAYLIST (PART TWO)

1. J.C. Fogerty and Creedence Clearwater Revival – "Ramble Tamble" (1970) from *Cosmo's Factory* 7:11

I enjoyed Fogerty's "Bayou" rock guitar sound when I was a senior in high school. This piece represents his best guitar work in my opinion. It reminds me so much of Scotty Moore's playing back in the mid 50's for Elvis.

2 Robert Fripp and King Crimson – "Prince Rupert's Lament" from *Lizard* (1970) 2:30

No one can play guitar like Fripp. This piece, from 1970's Lizard, is very much ahead of its time. Fripp's serpentine guitar makes for a very mystical musical experience here.

3. Mark Farner and Grand Funk Railroad – "Inside Looking Out" (1970) 9:30

Raw and unadulterated – straight out of the garage… that is, in a nutshell, the guitar style of Mark Farner. Invariably, he would play with his shirt off and assault his guitar with some of the hottest licks I had ever heard (when I was 18). I was so smitten by this hard rock trio, that I bought the first four Grand Funk albums and dug them. But other guitar heroes appeared on the musical scene as time went by and I grew tired of Grand Funk's derivative sound by 1971. But it's great to hear these guys again today. I think this piece, though long, best captures Farner's raw but highly successful guitar sound.

4. John Lennon – "I Found Out" from *Plastic Ono Band* (1970) 3:30
He was perhaps the best "pure" rock and roll guitarist of them all. If I were a rock band producer and I needed a great rhythm rock n' roll guitarist, someone who would provide a "kick ass" rock and roll bottom, I would hire John Lennon without hesitation. On this piece Lennon is at his understated best as "Guitar Hero." He may not have been the fastest or the most technical of rock guitarists, but he could "rock out," and this is his best piece in my opinion.

5. Jim McCarty and Cactus – "Parchman Farm" (1970) 6:20
Talk about pure energy on guitar, Jim McCarty takes the cake. He was the quintessence of "sweaty and speedy" guitar hero, run amok! "High Octane" best describes this guy.

6. Jeff Floro, with Stephen Lee – "Blood Was Its Avatar" (1972) 8:20.
Mike Moore- Organ; Dennis Foss- Drums. Recorded at Hoover Street.

What would Jeff F say if he knew that he had been included in a two day, organized listening seminar in the back hills of Santa Maria California, centering on the theme of the "Guitar Hero," along with the likes of Clapton, Hendrix, Page, etc? He would probably say: "Hey Boss, you gotta hear my new album!" Anyway, I thought Jeff could rock out back in the old days, so for the fun of it, I include Jeff F on this list. In this recording, Jeff ironically is not playing an electric guitar per se, but an electric bass. I chose this jam because I feel it truly shows Jeff's strong technical ability as a rock guitarist, albeit bass guitarist.

7. Dickie Betts and the Allman Brothers Band – "Jessica" (1973) 4:00
I've always been a fan of the Allman Brothers' Southern Rock sound, and the guy mostly responsible for that sound was guitarist Dickie Betts, and not Duane Allman. This piece is my favorite from that era.

8. Jimmy Page and Led Zeppelin – "The Rover" (1975) from *Physical Graffiti* 5:36
Now for a powerhouse. I rank Jimmy Page #2 on my List of Great Guitar Heroes. This piece just overpowers the listener (if played loudly). Imagine hearing Page play it live. My favorite of all the Led Zeppelin pieces.

9. Lonesome Dave Peverett and Foghat – "Slow Ride" (1977) 8:00
This piece (ironic title notwithstanding) is anything but slow. Lonesome Dave, formerly of Savoy Brown, is the main driver of this "rock out" jam session. Are you ready?

10. Kurt Cobain and Nirvana – "In Bloom" from *Nevermind* (1991) 4:17
Kurt would probably be insulted that I would skip so many years, from 1977 to 1991, and include him on this "Guitar Hero" list. But if you ask any young person from age 13 to 33, they will tell you their musical hero is Kurt Cobain. I think this piece kicks some serious rock ass. Excellent guitarist in my opinion.

11. Chuck Berry – "Sweet Little Sixteen" (1957) 2:30
I end this musical odyssey of guitar gods with "Zeus" himself.

PLAYLIST #2
"THE SAXOPHONE AND THE HUMAN VOICE"

FOR THIS LISTENING EXPERIENCE, I have chosen specially selected music featuring two instruments that I have been exploring lately: The "sonorous" saxophone and perhaps the greatest instrument ever devised— the human voice. Except for one avant-garde, progressive rock piece by King Crimson, and a great jazz piece by Count Basie, these are serious, highly sophisticated, sometimes intensely spiritual, concert pieces; from the antiquated Gregorian Chant of the first millennium, to the amazing, 19th century choral sounds of Rachmaninoff, to the dazzling Impressionistic intonations of Claude Debussy, to the relatively modern musical landscapes of Edison Denisov, Gyorgy Ligeti and Darius Milhaud. I hope you will enjoy this playlist of beautiful, spiritually-edifying sounds.

1. "Christe Redemptor;" Gregorian Chant, (2:27) (1st Millennium)
Sung by the Monks of the Benedictine Abbey en Calcat with the Boy's Choir from L'Alumnat.

This reminds me of my days in Catholic school back in the 60's. Father Vincent Molthen was my music teacher back then, and I credit him for turning me on to the "classics," especially choral classics. This piece showcases the haunting but ebullient sound of the "Male" voice, both adult and adolescent. In my mind's eye, I can almost see humble monks in a "dark ages" cathedral, cloistered together, as the "Black Death" ravages the countryside beyond those safe walls.

2. Debussy, Rhapsody for Orchestra and Alto Saxophone, (10:06) 1908

Performed by the Philharmonia Orchestra, with Theodore Kerkezoz on Sax.

    I first heard this masterpiece back in 1975 when I bought the Nonesuch recording at Lovell's. This is an excellent rendition of this rousing impressionistic soundscape by one of the best composers in music history. Again, the saxophone has "sonorous" qualities that no other musical instrument can match.

3. Debussy, "Sirenes," from *Nocturnes* (10:08) 1893—1898

Eugene Ormandy and the Philadelphia Orchestra

    A beautiful piece by Maestro Debussy. Here we have the hypnotic, but fatal female voices of the mythological Sirens from Homer's epic poem – The Odyssey. As foretold by the witch, Circe, no seafaring Argonaut has every survived hearing the voices of these gorgeous witches, without being magically drawn to their rocks, and drowning as their foundering boat goes under the roaring surf. In order to hear this amazing singing and still survive, the hero Odysseus has himself tied to the mast of his ship, while his rowing shipmates have wads of beeswax stuck inside their ears, and as a result, are not drawn to the rocks by the Sirens. And so, according to legend, Odysseus is the only mortal to survive this musical encounter. Athena, his patron goddess, was indeed with him on that long-ago day. And now we too can enjoy their compelling music, and live to tell about it.

4. Milhaud, Darius; "Scaramouche: Suite for Alto Saxophone and Orchestra," Composed in 1937 (9:48) 3 Movements.
Same performers as #2

What a great saxophone piece this is. I especially like the last movement, with its Latin overtones. The second movement is quite beautiful and simple. I played this so often last summer, I can now whistle every note by heart. Definitely one of my favorites.

5. Di Lasso, Orlando, (1532-1594) "Timor Et Tremor" (6:03), performed by the Choir of Trinity College, Cambridge
Listen as the voices in this piece practically climb over each other, building layer upon layer of sublime sounds. This is very cool Renaissance music from the time of Shakespeare, Michelangelo and the Medicis. Pure genius.

6. Count Basie and his Orchestra, with Lester Young on tenor sax. "Lester Leaps In" Recorded live September, 1939. (3:30)
Lester Young was and still is the "Master of the Sax" as far as pure musicianship is concerned. This Jazz virtuoso somehow played his instrument sideways, and he made it look and sound easy.

7. Rachmaninov, Sergei, "Bless the Lord, O My Soul," from *Vespers*, movement #2 (4:43) composed in 1882. Performed by the St. Petersburg Cappella
This is my favorite movement from the Vespers. Most of my life I associated Rachmaninov with passionate Russian piano music, but much to my surprise and delight, I read about this amazing choral work by "the Rock," and decided to buy it. I was not disappointed. If this doesn't get you in touch with your inner soul, then nothing will.

8. Ibert, Jacques, "Concertino for Alto Sax and 11 Instruments," (12:03)
Composed in 1935 (3 movements) Performed by the same artists in #'s 2 &4.
   I like this piece immensely, mainly because of the Jazz influence, but mostly because it was composed with one of my all-time favorite composers in mind – Maurice Ravel. Neo-classical in style, I especially like the middle slow movement. The last movement requires amazing virtuosity to bring it off.

9. Ligeti, Gyorgy; "Magany" and "Ket Kanor" (two movements) composed in 1946 (5:36)

Performed by the London Sinfonietta Voices, conducted by Terry Edwards.

Mystical and abstract, this is a very compelling work by one of the best choral composers of the 20th Century. Taken from obscure Hungarian folk music, this is among the finest ever composed by Ligeti. If you've ever seen 2001, A Space Odyssey, you may remember hearing two of Ligeti's choral works, especially the bizarre voices when the stone monolith appears.

10. Denisov, Edison; "Sonata for Alto Sax and Piano," (12.00) Composed in 1970.

Performed by the BBC National Orchestra of Wales; Claude Delangle on Saxophone.

This Sonata is in 3 movements; the first being an overture, the second is an interesting solo for Sax that leads right into the finale. You can also pick up on some jazz elements in the last movement. I especially like the juxtaposed piano in this piece; it brings some buoyancy and shape to it.

11. Holtz, Gustav, "Neptune," from *The Planets* Op. 32 (6:47) composed in 1916.

Performed by the Boston Symphony Orchestra, William Steinberg, Conductor.

I first heard The Planets on the radio one early morning back in 1971 as I was driving to my 7 am History class at Rio Hondo. "Wow," I said to myself, "this is great music. I've got to go to Lovell's today to get it." And of course I did. I bought the LP version of this CD – the Boston Orchestra version, which I consider to be the definitive one. When I first played "Neptune," I couldn't believe how mystical and gorgeous it was. Never has the human voice sounded more compelling.

12. King Crimson, "Formentera Lady" from *Islands* (1971) (7:00)

I chose this piece for this list because not only is it great music, but it utilizes both Voice and Sax so powerfully and uniquely.

13. Schubert, Franz, "Ave Maria," from *Fantasia*, produced by Walt Disney in 1940 (6:00)

Performed by the Philadelphia Orchestra, conducted by Leopold Stokowski.

I end this session with a video excerpt from Disney's Fantasia. It is the "Ave Maria" sung with spiritual aplomb and with accompanying animation.

PLAYLIST #3
"THE BEST IN 'LIVE' MUSIC"

AS A RELATIVELY YOUNG aficionado of rock music back in the early 1970's, I would make my once-a-week journey to Lovell's Record Store in Uptown Whittier with at least a 5 dollar bill in my pocket. And what did I usually buy back in those good old days of my 18th year on this planet? "Live" recordings of my favorite groups, like Cream, Johnny Winter, and The Who, and I especially dug the *Woodstock* soundtrack.
But I tend to think it was the Cream's *Wheels Of Fire* LP that first stoked my interest in "Live" records. The sheer spontaneity of it all enthralled me greatly; I couldn't believe Toad was over 15 minutes long, and it was mostly a drum solo. To me, this was totally cool because while listening to this piece full blast on my turn table in my humble bedroom on Hoover Street, I felt as if I were actually at the Fillmore, watching one of the greatest rock trios jam their asses off. This and all the other "Live" recordings I procured during that time gave me much more emotional satisfaction than their "studio" counterparts.

These "Live" recordings were actually historical events in some cases, like the aforementioned Woodstock LP. While others were simply great gigs caught unaltered on tape. I also enjoyed the longer playing time of these recordings because it gave the various musicians time to strut their technical stuff. Some of the best virtuoso playing I have ever heard all emanate from "Live" recordings. I suppose it makes a difference if a musician has a crowd of 10 to 20 thousand screaming fans staring at him, or in the case of Woodstock, over a half million people.

MIND TAVERN

PLAYLIST (PART ONE)

1."With A Little Help From My Friends," Joe Cocker and the Grease Band, from *Woodstock* (7:00) August, 1969.
I start this part with a DVD recording of what I consider to be the single greatest "Live" recorded performance I have ever seen or heard. When I first saw Joe Cocker's scintillating performance on the film, Woodstock, I was completely bowled over. Even though the Grease Band provides some cheesy backing vocals, Cocker's incomparable vocal on this Beatles' cover deserves an Academy Award for Best Performance by a Singer. The eerie organ tones bring back a million memories for me. And as for Cocker's ending on this recording, well, it can only be seen and heard to be believed.

2. " Mona," Quicksilver Messenger Service, from *Happy Trails* (6:53) recorded at the Fillmore West, 1968.
I first heard this Live recording of Quicksilver on KNAC – FM radio back in January of 1970. Thank goodness for FM radio back in those early days. It was on this station that I heard many outrageous "Live" recordings that would sometimes go on for ten minutes! AM radio didn't do that! I play it today because I still enjoy its understated quality, and the deliberate guitar work is still amongst my favorites with regard to "Live" performances. When was the last time you heard any Quicksilver? Great vintage psychedelic rock from "Hippie Mecca" – San Francisco.

3. "Stormy Monday," Mountain, from *The Great Music Festivals of the 1970's*, (15:00) recorded July 4, 1970 at the Atlanta Pop Festival.
I believe I have played this particular recording at least 300 times in my life. Mountain didn't stay together for very long, but while they were together, they produced some fine cutting edge jams. Lead guitarist Leslie West just rocks out in this jam, and one can also appreciate the fine bass guitar of Felix Papalardi, ex-producer of Cream. I used to get up and dance to this one.

4. "You Don't Love Me," Allman Brothers Band, from *At The Fillmore East* **(19:16) recorded March, 1971**
Definitely the best cut from one of the best Live recordings every made, at least according to many of the writers I have perused down through the years. The recording quality is simply unsurpassed, and this has to be Duane Allman's finest musical moment. The sales clerk from Lovell's recommended this LP to me back in 1972, and he wasn't wrong when he said it was "righteous."

5. "Magic Bus," The Who, from *Live At Leeds* **(7:00) recorded 1970 in England.**
I know, everyone feels The Who's best LP is Who's Next. But I beg to differ. Of all their LP's, this one – *Live at Leeds* – is the most interesting and the most musically "Real". Pete Townsend's Lead guitar on this and Keith Moon's drumming are amazingly tight and just plain exciting. I can only imagine what it must have been like to have been present in England all those years ago when The Who broke the Guinness record for being the loudest rock band in history. A great jam for the ages.

6. "Stepping Out," Cream, recorded at The Winterland in San Francisco, March, 1968 (3:29)
I have always enjoyed Cream's "Live" recordings; In fact, I feel the band was more suited for "Live" recordings than "Studio" in my opinion. There is nothing finer than a good Clapton jam with Ginger and Jack backing him up. Musical pyrotechnics at its best. This piece builds up to a shattering electrical climax; one of Clapton's best "Live" performances that I have heard.

PLAYLIST (PART TWO)

1. *Pictures at an Exhibition* **(Promenade, The Hut of Baba Yoga, The Curse of Baba Yoga, The Hut of Baba Yoga, The Great Gates of Kiev) Emerson Lake and Palmer (20:00) recorded March, 1971 at Newcastle City Hall.**

Dennis F turned me on to this LP back in 1974, my last year of college. I had heard ELP on numerous occasions before, while riding in DF's Pinto to and from Coco's. And I admit I was quite impressed with Emerson's skills at the keyboard. But I took a special liking to this LP because of my interest in "Classical" music. The Russian composer Mussorgsky had already been one of my favorites when I first heard this ELP. So it wasn't difficult to listen to it and to like it. This is great music which should be heard with headphones on.

2. "Cold Turkey," John Lennon and the Plastic Ono Band from *Live Peace In Toronto* **– 1969 (3:43)**

I can recall jamming with RWB back in its infancy down in the basement, and taking tea breaks upstairs with Dave and Dennis in my bedroom. And while we drank tea and ate Twinkies, we listened to this "Live" LP by John and Yoko. Most of it, in my opinion, is shit, except for this great recording of the John Lennon piece – "Cold Turkey." Eric Clapton's lead guitar makes this piece great; it brings so much heft and validity to it. But as for Yoko's primal screams wafting in and out in the background, well, that is still hideous sounding. Side B of this LP is great for a good laugh.

3. "Room To Move," John Mayall from *The Turning Point* **(4:34) recorded July, 1969 at the Fillmore East, New York**

A friend brought over this LP to my Hoover Street pad one fine spring day in 1971, played "Room To Move" on my little stereo, and immediately I was struck by the virtuoso harmonica playing of John Mayall. I can recall feeling very jealous of Mayall's great playing ability, and this piece has remained one of my all-time favorites.

4. "Eight Miles High," The Byrds from *Untitled* (16:15) recorded in 1970 at Queen's College, New York.
I recall playing this LP over and over again in late 1970 inside my Hoover Street pad. It is simply a great jam (and recording) with Gram Parsons and Roger McGuinn leading the way.

5. "China Cat Sunflower," Grateful Dead, from *Europe '72*, (5:33)
This is true "Head" music, par excellence. Jerry Garcia and his very cool band perform most excellently in this Live recording from 1972. The piece is from their triple album, Europe '72, which is probably their most popular album, at least according to total sales. This music is very cool, and is highly recommended.

6. "The Celebration of the Lizard," The Doors from *Absolutely Live* (14.14) recorded in 1969
I end my playlist with this great Rock Opera — starring the Lizard King, Jim Morrison. When the Doors made their debut in the late 60's, no one had ever heard anything like them before because of their fusion of rock music and poetry. The Oedipal overtones and sexual imagery of his words are still spellbinding and hypnotic.

PLAYLIST #4
"BEST ALL-TIME ALBUM —ABBEY ROAD"

THERE IS ONLY ONE LP from my halcyon youthful days that I can honestly say the following about it: I love each and every song in it equally. I cannot say the same for any other LP that my ears have heard down through the years, and there are some great ones in my collection that not only changed the Rock landscape culturally, but also in a profound way, my own personal tastes in music as well. Those very few LP's that come to mind are: Wheels Of Fire by The Cream, The Beatles' Sgt. Peppers Lonely Hearts Club Band and the White Album, plus King Crimson's Larks Tongues In Aspic . Even these great albums have at least one piece I tend to skip when it plays on my CD player. With 'Wheels, it's "Pressed Rat And Warthog" (Were they serious when they recorded this lemon?). With Sgt. Peppers it has to be "Good Morning Good Morning," which is to me a complete pain in the ear; With The White Album, I still find John Lennon's "Revolution 9" a bit obscure and a big waste of vinyl space that could have included maybe three or four great songs instead; And with Lark's Tongues, the greatest of all progressive rock albums in my humble opinion, it would have to be "Exiles." (After an interesting beginning with mellotron and miscellaneous sound effects, it unfortunately unravels into a mediocre vocal piece by John Wetton, with David Cross' syrupy violin backing him). But with regard to The Beatles' Abbey Road every song is a pure delight to listen to; in fact, I have played this LP so often in my life, that I have involuntarily committed to memory practically every single word in the lyrics to every song.

MIND TAVERN

SIDE ONE

1. Come Together – (4:20)

John's best contribution to this LP. His vocal has the perfect pitch and cadence; a true rocker with great lyrics. And the electric piano by the invisible Beatle – Billy Preston, adds so much to this classic piece. I can recall going to an 'end of semester' dance in early 1970 on the outside basketball courts at Whittier High. The dance was called "Come Together," named after the hottest song playing on the radio airwaves at the time. Randy J's band was playing on the blacktop, and mostly they played Led Zeppelin—a big disappointment since they didn't play any Beatles.

2. Something – (3:02)

This is definitely George Harrison's most commercially successful song. The orchestral background gives this piece its richness of tone and its unforgettable quality. And George's brief guitar solo adds the perfect touch. You can't get much better than this.

3. Maxwell's Silver Hammer – (3:28)

I still regard Paul as the undisputed leader of the Beatles, even with two of them dead. Why? Because of his astonishing eclecticism as a song writer. Whereas John was, by his own admission, primarily a 'Rock 'n Roller, Paul, on the other hand, can not be pigeon-holed in this way, having written so many different types of music; something for everybody as the saying goes. This is one of those fun-filled pieces that an 8 year old child could appreciate. Listen for the Moog making its debut in the music of The Beatles; played tastefully by a session dude named Mike Vickers.

4. Oh! Darling – (3:27)

Another Paul McCartney masterpiece. His vocal is so Elvis-like and so emotionally rendered, it leaves me almost breathless, and speechless I might add.

5. Octopus's Garden – (2:51)
Ringo's turn to add to the brilliance. Talk about benign. This piece is so hygienically recorded, one could eat one's dinner off its waves of sound and not get botulism poisoning. "Oh what joy for every girl and boy!" Quite a contrast from today's toxic lyrics and mind-melting tidal waves of unabashed electric noise.

6. I Want You (She's So Heavy) – (7:47)
In his Rolling Stone interview of 1970, John stated that Abbey Road "had no life in it." I beg to disagree. Just listen to this dynamic rock masterpiece. John's vocal and guitar are perfectly complimented as this piece soars for an amazing 7 minutes. Of course the ending was and is so cool; it builds up to an ever-increasing crescendo, then like an abrupt death in the family, it ends with no warning— a foreshadowing perhaps of things to come. The guitar solo in the middle is literally beautiful, and John's primal scream is unforgettable. Another foreshadowing?

7. Here Comes The Sun – (3:06)
I believe George had reached his song-writing zenith with Abbey Road. This piece is simply a masterpiece. Ringo provides a steady satisfying beat, and the lyrics just resonate as you listen. As for the guitar work, well, what can I say? Pure magic!

8. Because – (2:46)
Beautiful lyrics and sublime singing here. It is simply a great piece of music. Want to hum along? It will elevate your soul indeed!

SIDE TWO – SUITE OF BEATLES' MINIATURE CLASSICS

9. You Never Give Me Your Money – (4:03)
Another "Paul piece" that has a very interesting transition in it— from a

light and airy torch song to a rollicking rock paean to the ending 60's. "1 2 3 4 5 6 7, all good children go to heaven." Well, I always go to "music heaven" listening to this very cool piece.

10. Sun King – (2:26)
Beautiful guitar playing and singing; so simple and inspiring. And John's singing is so unlike him. It is actually nice to listen to. I'm sure he probably hated it while alive, but I love it.

11. Mean Mister Mustard – (1:06)
A very cool, knee-slapping piece that stands out as one of my favorites on this LP. Too bad it isn't a longer more developed piece. I'm pretty sure this one is a "John" piece. Ringo's drumming adds so much to this.

12. Polythene Pam – (1:13)
Again we can hear John singing this one. I looked up "polythene" in the dictionary. and it's not there. I do know what "poly" means, but the "thene" part, I have no clue about that. That's John for you. Ever eccentric and mysterious. And obscure.

13. She Came In Through The Bathroom Window – (1:59)
One of Paul's more memorable pieces, and one of the great cover songs by Joe Cocker. The lyrics are somewhat farcical too. "She could steal but she could not rob" Okay Paul, I can dig it.

14. Golden Slumbers – (1:31)
Another "Paul" piece with exquisite orchestration. "Golden Slumbers fill your eyes," sings Paul. To me these golden slumbers fill my soul with effable joy.

15. Carry That Weight – (1:36)
It begins and ends with seamless transitions. Just think how great these

pieces could have been had they been individual songs at least three minutes each. Their greatness is so short-lived— I guess like The Beatles themselves.

16. The End – (2:22)
Definitely my favorite interlude from the Suite. Ringo's drumming is so excitingly tight, and the three distinctive guitar solos; first Paul, then George, and finally John (like they're in competition to out-do each other). Well, it's just an amazing swan jam by the Fab Four. If I were George Martin and present the day this was recorded, I would've told the Fab Four to jam longer; perhaps another 2 or 3 minutes. Why stop a good thing?

17. Her Majesty – (0:25)
This is an odd but delightful coda to this amazing LP.

PLAYLIST #5
"MUSICAL OBSESSIONS"

THE FOLLOWING PIECES represent to me those short-lived musical obsessions that I experienced throughout my life at one time or another. Who knows how these things begin. I guess I would initially hear the piece on the radio or on an LP or CD and I instantly developed a relationship with it. I would figuratively play the piece to death; perhaps for an entire month; sometimes for a couple weeks. And most times my obsessions would last a shorter time, like 2 to 3 days. But at any rate, it seems my entire life is seamed together by one musical obsession after another; like a lifeline from the glorious world of music to my own real world of work, stress and schedules. Obviously 90 minutes is not nearly enough time to play everything I have loved during my life. So I narrowed everything down to these 17 pieces; very eclectic indeed— from John Field, the classical "father" of the etude piano piece, to the interesting modernist music of Jocelyn Pook. And it is with SHE, that I begin my List of Musical Obsessions.

1. "Migrations," Jocelyn Pook, 1999, from the *Eyes Wide Shut* soundtrack, (3:46)
I first heard this interesting musical excursion when I watched Stanley Kubrick's fascinating last film, Eyes Wide Shut in 2001. The otherworldly voices and the ever-increasing crescendo of manic sounds in this work is most compelling.

2. "The Family And The Fishing Net" Peter Gabriel from *Security*, 1982 (7:00)

For the longest time I was pissed off at the artist Peter Gabriel for bailing on one of my favorite progressive rock groups of the 1970's: Genesis. And so, I chose to ignore his early solo work for quite a few years. A personal boycott if you will. Of course I eventually came to my senses when I heard a recording of his Live concert at the Whiskey in 1977. (We used to sit around Dennis F's pad on Broadway Street and play that concert over and over again. And that is when I developed a strong appreciation for Gabriel "en solo.") This is the most interesting piece from his Security CD. Excellent vocal and thought-provoking lyrics.

3. "B'Boom" King Crimson from *Thrak* 1995 (4:11)

Bill Bruford's drum solo in this piece is absolutely enthralling. I always knew he was the best, bar none, from all the listening Dennis F and I did back in the 70's when Crimson came out with their best LP's: Lark's Tongues, Starless and Red. This piece is definitely the most interesting from *Thrak*.

4. "Drugs," This Mortal Coil from *Filigree & Shadow* 1986 (3:11)

Dennis F turned me on to This Mortal Coil back in the mid to late 90's with an inclusion in one of his very cool cassette compilations. A very unique and eclectic assortment of sounds emanates from this very creative band. I like "Drugs" because it is so bold, different, and its brazen sounds take hold of your ears uncompromisingly. Kick Ass rock!

5. "Only The Strong,' Midnight Oil from *"10, 9, 8, …."* 1983 (4:32)

I rarely play Midnight Oil any more, but back in the late 80's I was very impressed with their swagger and Neo-Punk approach to rock music. I first saw this group on MTV back in 1984, and recorded "Only The Strong." I recall that I thoroughly enjoyed their very different sound; at least in comparison to all the "New Wave" and Michael Jackson music predominating at that time.

6. "Midi in E major: Allegretto" John Field (music composed in 1836) (4:10)
John Field is the most under-rated, under-heard and forgotten Romantic composer of all time! And that is a shame. Yes, Beethoven was and is the quintessence of "Romanticism," but take a listen to this 4 minute masterpiece by a truly remarkable composer of pure musical loveliness. A+ in my grade-book. This recording is performed by John O'Connor on the Telarc label, 1990, entitled "Nocturnes of John Field." Highly recommended.

7. "Traintime" The Cream from *Wheels Of Fire* 1968 (3:38)
Jack Bruce of Cream could sing well, play Bass with the best of them and he could play a wicked harmonica as well. This piece is my favorite from the seminal LP of the late 60's: Wheels Of Fire by The Cream. I must've played this piece at least a thousand times during the Summer of 1969, and I never tired of it. It influenced me to buy a harmonica and start playing it. Outstanding fusion of blues and rock.

8. "So Rare," Jimmy Dorsey 1957 (2:35)
In 1957 I was 5 years old and very excited about the music of Elvis Presley. Who wasn't at the time? In fact, "Teddy Bear" was constantly playing on the radio and on my brother's little 45 record player. However, there was another 45 record I played to death that summer— So Rare, by the Jimmy Dorsey Orchestra. I still love the interesting blend of saxophone sounds and voices in this piece, and in a way it is a sad work to listen to, for this little gem by Dorsey was one of the last vestiges of the Big Band sound from the 40's, before Rock 'N Roll completely took over the "Musical World."

9. "Mother Tongue," Dead Can Dance from *The Serpent's Egg*, 1988 (5:15)
Another band introduced to me by Dennis F in the mid-90's. Every piece on Dead Can Dance's Serpent's Egg is fascinating to listen to. However, my

favorite is "Mother Tongue." Listen to the incessant, extremely dynamic percussion in this piece as it sweeps you beyond the facades. I guess all of us have a little slice of the "primeval" in us, residing deeply in our sub-consciousness. This piece appeals to the tamed animal in all of us.

10. "Fast Life Rider," Johnny Winter from *Second Winter,* 1969 (7:01)

I first heard Johnny Winter in the Spring of 1970 while recording stuff off of KNAC- FM radio, and simply put, I was amazed at his guitar virtuosity. In fact, for a while there in the early 70's, I thought Winter was better, technically-speaking, than Hendrix. "Fast Life Rider," indeed, rocks out. The incessant drum rolls acts as a background grid for Winter's extended solo; a solo replete with fuzz and wah-wah effects. And his speed still amazes me to this day.

11. "1983…(A Merman I Should Turn To Be)," Jimi Hendrix Experience from *Electric Ladyland* 1968 (13:39)

Speaking of guitar virtuosity, Jimi Hendrix cannot be left off this playlist. For I experienced numerous obsessions of his transcendent music back in the late 60's. This one, an extended, but very subtle, musical journey to the bottom of the ocean, is a gorgeous "tour de force" most Hendrix aficionados overlook.

12. *Fantasien Op. 116* Intermezzo "Adagio," Johannes Brahms, composed in 1891 (3:52)

I discovered the poignant and highly emotional piano music of Brahms in 1975. Dennis F and I would comb through the classical section at Lovell's in Uptown looking for obscure but interesting LP's. I found one by Brahms that included this 4 minute Intermezzo. Listen and enjoy its mellifluous, cascading, highly charged sounds. William Congreve, the English playwright, once wrote: "Music hath charms to soothe the savage beast or bend a knotted oak." Well, if that is so, than this piece "hath such charms." It is perhaps Brahms' most beautiful work of art. This recording is from a Philips CD, performed by Stephen Kovacevich in 1983.

13. "Summa for Strings," Arvo Pärt, from *Fratres* composed in 1978 (4:16)

I discovered the fascinating music of Arvo Pärt in the late 90's when I first heard "Fratres" on a CD compiled by the musicologist, Thomas Moore. This movement, "Summa for Strings," is another charmer. Bright, crisp-sounding and very optimistic, I play this one whenever I feel down. I recommend anything by Pärt, especially his sacred vocal music.

14. "The First Day," Anuna 1993 (3:08)

In 1997 I watched Riverdance on PBS, the exuberant musical from Ireland, composed by Bill Whelan. And I was completely blown away. In that show there were two vocal pieces that caught my ear by a group of singers called Anuna, and I was suitably impressed with them from the very beginning. So therefore, I add some "ethnic" music to this list. Here we have some Celtic music for voices from their first CD that has a benign, hypnotic effect on the listener. Sacred and haunting, I love the flute rendering at the end of this.

15. "Starless And Bible Black," King Crimson from *Starless and Bible Black* 1974 (9:11)

Twisted, dark, insatiably consuming, this outrageous piece from King Crimson, circa 1974, epitomizes mid 70's progressive rock. Robert Fripp's winding, sinister, almost snake-like guitar playing dazzles. Bill Bruford on drums, David Cross on Mellotron and John Wetton on Bass miraculously hold up their ends with superb technical skill, to produce an electrifying, mind-bending rock piece, second to none, in my opinion, to anything being done, progressively, at that time. An absolute masterpiece.

16. "Through the Field I Took My Way," Gustav Mahler from *Songs of a Wayfarer* 1883 (4:00)

Cal-State Fullerton music professor, Dr. Burton Karson, turned me on to the sublime music of Gustav Mahler in the Fall of 1972 when he played this wonderful song in his "Music in Our Society" class one afternoon in October. I immediately fell in love with it. It is the second movement from what I believe is Mahler's most beautiful and haunting opus: "The Songs Of A Wayfarer." This version was recorded in 1985 on the EMI label by Sir John Barbirolli and the Halle' Orchestra. The solo vocal by Janet Baker may not be the all-time, definitive performance on tape, but it is nevertheless quite satisfying. A+

17. "I'm Crazy 'Bout My Baby," Fats Waller And His Rhythm (2:50) 1936

I end this playlist with the rollicking, rhythmic jazz piano of Fats Waller. Recorded during the height of the Great Depression, I can see why this guy and his very tight band were so popular back then. When I hear this, I am instantly transformed back in time to a simpler, but albeit, tentative era of time, when escaping reality was in vogue, and I still marvel at his brilliant piano-playing technique. There was nobody like him. His premature death at age 39 in 1943 robbed audiophiles of a plethora of fine, toe-tapping music.

PLAYLIST #6
"MUSICAL PIECES I HAVE ENJOYED DOWN THROUGH THE YEARS"

FOR THIS PLAYLIST, I combed through my LP collection and picked out some pieces that I have thoroughly enjoyed at one time or another since the 1960's. I hope you enjoy my offerings. With all respect, I give you this eclectic assortment of sounds:

1. **"Be My Love," Mario Lanza (circa 1958) Approx. 3:00**
In 1967 as a sophomore in high school, I recall experiencing a two month mania for the amazing opera singer, Mario Lanza. I had heard an old recording of Caruso that summer, and was enthralled by that tenor's startling power and range. When I first heard Mario Lanza's rendering of "Be My Love" on this old LP, I was suitably impressed and I even came to the conclusion that this was the greatest tenor I had ever heard in my whole life, even better than Caruso himself, and after many years of listening to other opera vocalists, I still think no one even comes close, even though I have greatly enjoyed listening to the contemporary blind vocalist Bocelli on numerous occasions. Sadly, Lanza died prematurely of heart disease at the young age of 38 in 1959.

2. **"Dust My Broom," written by Elmore James; played by Canned Heat,** *Live at the Topanga Corral,* **1967 (5:46)**
In 1971 I was a Canned Heat "freak." Dennis F will vouch for that claim. They were the best boogie band in the world, bar none. I picked up this LP at Lovell's in uptown Whittier for 3 bucks one summer morning, and

immediately dug the live stuff they did at the Topanga Corral during the "Summer of Love." Larry "The Mole" Taylor was, in my humble opinion, one of the best bassists in the business at that time. And lead guitarist, Henry Vestine, was solid too. This is simply some of the best, down and dirty, blues/boogie I have heard in my lifetime.

3. "Legend of a Mind," Moody Blues from *In Search Of The Lost Chord* 1968 (6:40)

"Timothy Leary's dead…" Definitely my favorite "Moody" piece of them all. Not that I was a disciple of the good Harvard professor or his LSD hype. This is just good music with interesting lyrics. The Moodys were consummate musicians and rarely did they come out with stinky albums. Enjoy this excursion back to 1968— a watershed year in American history.

4. "Exercise In C Major For Harmonica, Bass and Shufflers," John Mayall, from *Jazz Blues Fusion*, recorded Live, December, 1971. (8:10)

I bought this LP in the summer of 1972, right around the time I had my wisdom teeth pulled. Whenever I play this stuff, I experience psychic reactions; strange, reflexive remembrances of bloody sore gums and aching jaws. On the other hand, these sounds also bring back to mind images of the second love of my life – 16 year old Anna. The music is interesting too, with Blues and Jazz idioms being brought together by "Bluesbreaker" John Mayall, preeminent blues bassist, Larry Taylor of Canned Heat and four other jazz musicians I had never heard of when I bought this album. This is the best piece on the LP (in my opinion).

5. Debussy, "Danses Sacree Et Profane," (9:08) composed in 1903.

This very rich orchestration by French Impressionist, Claude Debussy, stands out as one of my all-time favorites. Harpist Marie-Claire Jamet and the French National Radio Orchestra do a splendid job in rendering this amazingly beautiful piece. It's interesting how certain pieces bring back vivid memories; I can recall playing this in the winter of 1975 in my old office on Hoover Street; it was a cold rainy night and I had the back door open, listening to the raindrops hitting the back yard pavement like thousands of miniature percussive drums. Dennis F would invariably drop by and we'd sit in the old office and play music for a few hours before driving out to Cocos. Those were indeed great days.

6. "Fascination Rag," from Take Five by Larry Fotine, recorded in stereophonic sound in 1958. (2:45)
In 1959 my parents purchased a "stereophonic" record player with two detachable speakers. They also bought this multi-colored "stereo" LP to play on their new stereo. I can recall the whole family sitting around this record player and being enthralled and amazed by the life-like sounds. Side A is an interesting tour around LA with Jack Wagner doing the narration. Side B contains just a smattering of short stereo pieces; one of which is this Dixieland Jazz specimen that is guaranteed to lift one's spirits. Cost of this new fangled LP back in 1959? $2.98. Expensive then, but a steal in today's high cost world.

7. "Valse Triste," composed by Jean Sibelius in 1903. Played by Leonard Bernstein and the New York Philharmonic Orchestra (5:03)
Of all the "Nationalistic" composers of the late 19th Century, Jean Sibelius stands out for being possibly the most patriotic in terms of musical composition. In his case, the country is Finland. It is debatable to state that no other composer in history had such a positive impact on the people of his homeland. This particular piece is a hauntingly beautiful tone poem, written for a patriotic play entitled "Kuolema" by the playwright, Armas Jarnefelt. I always get goosebumps when I listen to this masterpiece. It makes one want to go to Finland and soak up the local color there.

8. "Oh Lady, Be Good," written by the Gershwins; recorded by Count Basie and his Orchestra, October, 1936 in Chicago. (3:06)

Discovered by jazz enthusiast John Hammond while listening to the radio one evening, Kansas City's Count Basie was the best. Better than Duke Ellington. Better than Louis Armstrong. Better than Benny Goodman even. I know these are bold statements. And there is one reason why "The Count" stood out as the best jazz bandleader of all time. His name was Lester Young, probably the most outstanding saxophonist in the history of American jazz. This is an amazing recording by a true artist. Oh, to have been there that night in Chicago. I'm sure the jazz aficionados present were simply blown away, and not by "reefer" either.

9. "La Vaquilla," recorded in the late 1960's by El Mariachi Aguila De Guadalajara Mexico (3:30 approx.)

What can I say? I learned to appreciate Mexican "ethnic" music when I was 17 years old with these robust, Latin sounds. My mother, I might add, thought I was "off my rocker" back in 1969 when playing this LP instead of Jimi Hendrix. My interest in Mexican Mariachi music has been stroked recently with the Mexican workers at my house the past 3 months, who are adding on 500 square feet of living space. These workers are amazing. They have done a fantastic job, sawing and nailing incessantly, while playing their CD's of very cool Mariachi music. Even my daughters like this stuff now. Listening to this makes me hungry for Carne Asada.

10. "Can't Take It With You," from *Pyramid* by the Alan Parsons Project, 1978 (5:06)

Calvin P turned me on to this LP when he lived in his little crawlspace of an apartment in Whittier back in 1978. In fact I liked this LP so much, it was the only music I played during the entire summer of '78. On numerous occasions down through the years I have played this piece for my English students because of the interesting lyrics. The music is compelling too.

11. "Under Heavy Manners," from *God Save The Queen*, by Robert Fripp 1979 (5:14)

The final piece for this playlist is an interesting "Frippertronic" reaction to Robert Fripp's growing distaste for commercialized progressive rock and disco, musical genres that were reaching their almost derivative zenith by the time this LP came out in 1979. This unusual rendering was recorded in Calgary, Canada, with Buster Jones on bass, Paul Duskin on drums and Absalm el Habib on vocal. The words and guitar effects belong to Mr. Fripp himself.

PLAYLIST #7
"CLASSIC COUNTRY, MAHLER AND STRAVINSKY"

FOR THIS PARTICULAR PLAYLIST, I divided up 90 minutes of playing time into 3 segments. Segment One includes 15 minutes of classic Country Western hits from the 1950's and early 60's that I personally recall as a child, while traveling the western states with my family in a '58 Chevy Impala, with all those great songs emanating from the radio speaker on the front dashboard.

The second segment is 30 minutes and includes the playing of two pieces from two LP's that I used to play regularly as a college student back in the early 70's. And to conclude this playlist, I would like to present 45 minutes of the best of Igor Stravinsky, at least in my opinion. Without a doubt, the Petrushka is his tour de force masterpiece, and so I present the 1911 (composed) version in its entirety, with Igor himself at the baton. And to finalize my tribute to this great composer, I highly recommend the video of Alexis Weissenberg at the piano in 1965 performing Stravinsky's 1924 three movement piano transcription of Petrushka. It is well worth seeing this amazing performance.

SEGMENT I – "CLASSIC COUNTRY MEMORIES" (LATE 50'S TO THE MID 60'S)

1. "El Paso," Marty Robbins; recorded in 1959; (Approx. 4 minute)
Definitely my all-time favorite country western hit from those great days of the late 50's. I can recall traveling through Colorado, Montana, Oregon

and all the other western states during the summer of 1959 with my family, as we drove through endless vistas in the old '58 Chevy Impala. My father in particular loved this piece and would play it over and over again on his record player, even in his retirement years as he approached the end of his life. I can also recall my mother turning up the old radio inside the car when this song came on as we drove across the Golden Gate Bridge in San Francisco that long ago summer, and no one was permitted to talk until the piece was over. It was that great of a song.

2. "Pick Me Up On Your Way Down," Charlie Walker; recorded in 1958; (approx. 2:30)
Another classic from my childhood inside the '58 Impala. Again, my father was the one who loved this country classic from a time when life seemed replete with endless possibilities and optimism; American society was on the threshold of a new grand age, an epoch of unprecedented financial growth, suburban nirvana (with Tiki torches), outer space exploration and broad social justice on a national level. But of course, as a dumb kid of 6 years, I had no idea what was about to happen in the coming years of the 60's, but I still dug this song, even though I was a big Rock n' Roll fan at the time.

3. "The Three Bells," The Browns; recorded in 1959; (2:45)
I can recall hearing this sad song for the first time in the back seat of the Impala as we drove at sunset through central California on Highway 101 in the summer of '59. We were on our way to Buellton from San Francisco and I can remember having supper at the Anderson's Split Pea restaurant. My mother, many years later, told me about what happened that evening when the waitress asked me if I wanted any split pea soup with my dinner, and apparently upon hearing this natural question, I made a disgusted face, grunted loudly and said "Pea Soup? No!" Of course I thought it was another kind of "pee" soup. Amazing the memories a simple song like this can bring back after all these years.

4. "May The Bird Of Paradise Fly Your Nose," "Little" Jimmy Dickens; recorded in 1965, (2:20)

A great country classic from the mid 60's. I remember cruising up to Las Vegas with my parents in the winter of '66, up highway 15 through the desert in my dad's 1965 Chevy Impala and hearing this on the radio, We stayed at the old El Morocco Inn, there on The Strip, and I basically watched television as my parents gambled. I love the guitar in this piece and of course the rollicking vocal by "Little" Jimmy.

5. "Crazy," Patsy Cline; recorded in 1962, (2:40)

This is Patsy Cline at her best before her demise in an airplane crash. The accompanying piano is played expertly in this, adding the perfect touch. Listen carefully to Patsy, as she brilliantly renders a truly classic performance. In thinking back to the first time I heard this, I recall I was in the Impala; my father was driving us to St. Mary's Church on a Sunday morning. We were driving down Pickering Street, past the Siewart-Barber Funeral Home and the Safeway supermarket, when I first heard this masterpiece of early '60's country music. My dad turned up the radio as we turned into the St. Mary's parking lot for 9 o'clock Mass.

6. "Walkin' After Midnight," Patsy Cline, recorded in 1957, (2:30)

I end this segment with a reprise of Patsy Cline in her absolute prime as the Queen of Country. I was in my father's '54 Chevy sedan when I first heard this masterpiece. We were in line at the Sundown Drive-In theater and we had on radio station KFWB when my mother remarked how gorgeous Patsy Cline's singing voice was. And as a dumb kid, I had to agree. In fact, I agreed with everything my mother said. Only my brother thought Patsy Cline stunk.

MIND TAVERN

SEGMENT II — "THE TWO LPS"

7. Mahler, Symphony No. 2 "Resurrection," Eugene Ormandy, The Philadelphia Orchestra; Birgit Finnila, Contralto vocalist. (15:07) from Mahler's Greatest Hits (RCA) 1971.

This is the second time I have shared the amazing music of Gustav Mahler. For this playlist, I include the majestic 2nd Symphony, nicknamed the "Resurrection." While Mahler had to work hard to pay his bills with winter and spring conducting positions, he spent his off-summers composing some of the greatest music ever to come out of Western Europe around the turn of the 20th Century. His symphonies are personal quests for the essential truths of life and death. His music is at times screaming with pain and anguish. But at other times there is undeniable victory and redemption. These amazing orchestrations epitomize man's struggle with life and destiny. And it is categorically gorgeous. I recommend Symphonies 1, 2, 3, 4, 8 and 9 and his "Songs of a Wayfarer" if you wish to hear more of his inspiring, extraordinary sounds.

8. Haydn, "Concerto in E flat for Trumpet and Orchestra," Helmut Wobisch, trumpet; Antonio Janigro conducting I Solisti di Zagreb (13:57) composed circa 1796.

Franz Joseph Haydn was pure genius. In all his music there is his signature touch when the musical ideas go beyond mere beauty. There is a delight in listening to his music— like spooning chilled tapioca; you are moved to an ebullience only Haydn aficionados can understand. There is also a simplicity and an elegance to his symphonic pieces that transcend time. One can never grow tired of any of his masterpieces, and that includes this tour de force piece, no doubt written for his rich patrons – the Esterhazy family of Eisenstadt. Of all the Haydn pieces that I have heard since my college days, this is my favorite. Like all concerti, this piece is in 3 movements: Allegro (fast), Andante (slow) and Allegro (fast) again. This is indeed a treasure of music most people do not hear these days. A+

SEGMENT III – "STRAVINSKY AND HIS MASTERPIECE"

9. Stravinsky, "*Petrushka*," Igor Stravinsky conducting the Columbia Symphony Orchestra, 1911 Version; recorded in 1960. (approx. 30:00).
First of all this is amazing music; I have been listening to it regularly since 1990, and I still love the piece for its unique structure and overall aesthetics. Divided into 4 Tableaus or sections, this stirring ballet music was composed in the peaceful countryside while Stravinsky's sick wife was recuperating near Switzerland in 1910 to 1911. Stravinsky, too, was having his health issues during the creation of this piece; nicotine poisoning that laid him up for awhile. So, despite the setbacks in his personal life, he managed to create this extraordinary work of art that proved to be a commercial success. There are 15 distinct dance pieces, all centering around three principal characters (all puppets) during the Mardi Gras in St. Petersburg in the 1830's. The main character is a puppet ballerina by the name of *Petrushka*. But alas, it is not my intention to tell the entire scenario for this piece. Suffice it to say, listening to this piece all these years has truly enriched my life.

10. Stravinsky, "*Three Movements from Petrushka*," for piano. Alexis Weissenberg – piano. Recorded and filmed in 1965 by Ake Falck. (15:00)
Amazing virtuosity being displayed here. I have been playing this recording regularly for a year now, and would like to recommend its utter brilliance to all music lovers.

PLAYLIST #8
"COCKTAILS FOR THE SOUL"
POST WAR JAZZ OF THE 1950'S

THIS PARTICULAR THEME has been residing in the back of my mind like a caged cat for about 3 years. Now finally I have gotten this list together to share, and now the cat can be free at last. I became intensely interested in post World War 2 jazz after watching Ken Burns' fascinating documentary on PBS. I enjoyed learning about the roots of jazz and hearing the great sounds of Jelly Roll Morton, Sidney Bichet, Louis Armstrong, Duke Ellington, Billie Holiday, Chick Webb, Fletcher Henderson, Benny Goodman and Count Basie.

But what really caught my attention was the cool, be-bop jazz experimentations of the late 40's with Charlie "Bird" Parker and "Dizzy" Gillespie. I was completely blown away by their manic virtuosity on saxophone and trumpet, respectively. Then came the 1950's and innovators like Miles Davis, John Coltrane, Dave Brubeck, Milt Jackson, Paul Desmond, Art Tatum, Lionel Hampton, Thelonious Monk, Jimmy Smith, "Cannonball" Adderly and Curtis Fuller. That is when I became completely hooked on this greatest of all American exports— Jazz.

For this jazz playlist, I did not include Charlie Parker or Dizzy Gillespie. Even though their fabulous careers lasted well into the 50's, their best, definitive material, in my opinion, belongs primarily in the late 40's, when "Be-Bop" was all the rage in American Jazz, and I wanted to keep my focus for this list on the mid to late 50's. To lend some class and some variety to this list, I have also included pieces by four wonderful vocalists: Frank Sinatra, Ella Fitzgerald, Louis Prima and Keely Smith. The "Ella" piece, by the way, was recorded in February of 1960, which is still pretty damn close to the late 50's. She is just too unbelievably good to leave out.

One final note: The best part about doing this theme had to be my personal discovery of Miles Davis' classic album, Kind Of Blue. To think that I will have lived most of my life not having heard this sublime masterpiece greatly angers me. But I suppose that's the beauty of being a music aficionado; there is always a universe of music yet to be discovered. I can only surmise what other musical universes that are out there for all music fans to discover and enjoy. The discovering process is never-ending. So, without further ado my fellow musicologists, here are some very special musical cocktails for the soul:

1. The Modern Jazz Quartet, "Between The Devil And The Deep Blue Sea," (6:51) recorded in 1956. Milt Jackson- Vibes; John Lewis- Piano; Percy Heath- Bass; Connie Kay- Drums.
To start off my set, here is some very cool jazz from The Modern Jazz Quartet from 1956. Milt Jackson is, in my opinion, the best vibes player I have ever heard in this genre. When I hear this great music, I envision myself inside some dark downtown cocktail lounge on the lower east side of New York, and all around me are the denizens of the night, smoking cigarettes, drinking martinis and conspiring majestic moments in bed. And outside, the stars are out, with a neon cocktail sign beckoning the Devil to come inside for some great American jazz. "It is time to bid the devil good morning when you meet him." A+

2. The Dave Brubeck Quartet, "Blue Rondo A La Turk," from *Time Out*, 6:44 (1959) Dave Brubeck— Piano; Paul Desmond- Alto Saxophone; Eugene Wright- Bass; Joe Morello-Drums.
A fascinating jazz opus indeed. Brubeck's relentless theme music on piano drives this highly experimental piece. Paul Desmond's cool sax is nothing short of phenomenal. I especially enjoy the great interchange between bassist Eugene Wright and drummer Joe Morello. This piece, along with

"Take Five," pretty much epitomizes the California Jazz sound of the late 50's. The entire album is a classic and is highly recommended if you enjoy good, sophisticated modern jazz. It makes for great relaxed listening on a Sunday morning with a steaming cup of coffee. A+

3. The Tatum Group, "Somebody Loves Me," (7:10) recorded in 1955. Art Tatum— Piano; Lionel Hampton—Vibes; Harry Edison—Trumpet; Buddy Rich—Drums; Red Callender—Bass; Barney Kessel—Guitar.
More great jazz vibes from Lionel Hampton in 1955. And Art Tatum's piano just carries this masterwork with a fluid style that simply envelopes my soul like a sarong. Classic jazz for any occasion.

4. Thelonious Monk Quartet, with John Coltrane, "Bye-Ya," (6:31) recorded in 1957 at Carnegie Hall. Thelonious Monk—Piano; John Coltrane—Tenor Saxophone; Ahmed Abdul-Malik— Bass; Shadow Wilson— Drums.
Very experimental live jazz sounds from a concert at Carnegie Hall in 1957. Monk's piano style is bold, brazen and exciting. But what really makes this music shine is John Coltrane's exuberant saxophone. This music should be turned up so all can hear its soul-expanding textures in all its glory. Historic and amazing post-war jazz at its best.

5. Jimmy Smith, "Come On Baby," from *Home Cookin'* (6:48) recorded in 1959. Jimmy Smith—Organ; Percy France—Tenor Sax; Kenny Burrell—Guitar; Donald Bailey—Drums.
A friend turned me on to this album a few years ago while hanging out one day in Huntington Beach. Great organ is demonstrated here by Smith. It is so cool and stylistic; I again can't help but close my eyes and envision myself there, when this recording was made, sitting amidst the customers of a darkened jazz café, commiserating and lavishing upon this feast of sensual sounds.

6. Miles Davis, "All Blues," (11:13) recorded in 1959, from the album, *Kind Of Blue*. Miles Davis—Trumpet; John Coltrane—Tenor Saxophone; Julian "Cannonball" Adderly—Alto Sax; Bill Evans—Piano; Paul Chambers—Bass; Jimmy Cobb—Drums.

This is my favorite number from Miles Davis' landmark jazz album from 1959. What completely pisses me off about *Kind Of Blue* is that after being a music listener and collector for over 50 years, nearly two-thirds of my entire lifetime, I finally discovered it. Better late than never. It was like discovering a treasure chest in my back yard. I bought it in late March from Amazon and I was completely blown away by the rich, understated playing of Miles Davis on trumpet and especially John Coltrane on tenor sax. The other three musicians are fabulously great also. With regard to solos on this masterpiece: Miles goes first. "Amazing" is the only word I can think of to describe it. Then John Coltrane plays the second solo and is absolutely superb, followed by the masterful Cannonball Adderly on alto sax. Bill Evans expertly fills in throughout on piano. A true miracle of post war jazz, *Kind Of Blue* is now in my Top 3 of all-time favorite musical albums. I cannot recommend this album enough. A+

7. Ella Fitzgerald, "How High The Moon," (7:03) recorded in 1960 in Berlin, Germany, with Paul Smith on Piano, Jim Hall on Guitar, Wilfred Middlebrooks on Bass and Gus Johnson on Drums.

There is no way I can leave out the great and legendary Ella Fitzgerald from this post-war list. This is a very cool jam session from February of 1960 with some inspired singing on the part of Ella with her inimitable skat, be bop vocal style. Astonishingly controlled, no one could sing like her.

8. Frank Sinatra, "*In The Wee Small Hours Of The Morning*," Nelson Riddle Orchestra. (Approx. 4:00) recorded in 1955.

This is probably Sinatra's best vocal performance on what is considered by many critics to be his best, most personal album. Recorded shortly after his devastating divorce from Ava Gardner, you can't help but pick up on

Frank's deep, emotional sadness as he sings this amazing piece. Nelson Riddle does a superb job in backing up ol' "Blue Eyes" with some solid orchestration. This is the classic Sinatra album to explore and perhaps own. Highly recommended listening.

9. Louis Prima and Keely Smith, "That Old Black Magic," (3:00) recorded in 1958. Sam Butera— Tenor Sax.
I can recall my parents being very big fans of this pop / jazz vocal duo back in the late 50's. Whenever we took family vacations to Reno, Nevada or Lake Tahoe, they would schedule the trips around the performance dates of this hot jazz act. This was also a big hit in 1958 as it was played regularly on KFWB radio. "That old black magic has me in its spell." Evidently this song had a very powerful spell on my parents too.

10. John Coltrane, "Moment's Notice," from *Blue Train*," (9:06) recorded in 1957. John Coltrane- Tenor Sax; Lee Morgan- Trumpet; Curtis Fuller- Trombone; Kenny Drew- Piano; Paul Chambers-Bass; Philly Joe Jones- Drums.
I quote from the album sleeve of *Blue Train:* "John Coltrane has often been called a 'searching' musician. His literally wailing sound, spearing, sharp and resonant, creates what might be best described as an ominous atmosphere that seems to suggest a kind of intense probing into things far off, unknown and mysterious." Robert Levin (original liner notes). For me, this is just simply some very excellent, accomplished jazz that is emotionally satisfying and highly compelling. This is an astonishing album that must be owned by any jazz enthusiast. Again, this is highly recommended.

11. Dave Brubeck Quartet, "Take Five," from *Time Out* (5:24). Recorded in 1959. Paul Desmond on Alto Sax.
Another classic reprise from Brubeck's amazing jazz album, Time Out. I can recall listening to this on the radio as a kid and absolutely digging the

very cool saxophone solo by Paul Desmond. Hypnotic and intoxicating, I never grow tired of listening to this masterpiece. Cocktails anyone?

12. Miles Davis, "Flamenco Sketches," (alternate take) (9:12) Recorded in 1959 from *Kind of Blue*. Same musicians as with "All Blues"

Suffice it to say, if Jesus could play tenor saxophone, he would have played it like John Coltrane does on this. This is the alternate take of this piece and I can understand why the producers of this CD included it. Again, as with "All Blues," Miles has the first solo on trumpet. But unlike the aforementioned title, Cannonball takes the second solo on alto sax. It is funky and satisfying, but he merely paves the way for the incomparable John Coltrane, who makes the heavens weep with the third solo on tenor sax. It's hard to put in words just how beautiful his playing is. If only he had stayed off the drugs. Unfortunately, he had only 8 more years to live after making this tour de force album with Miles Davis.

13. The Modern Jazz Quartet, "Night In Tunisia" (6:08) Recorded in 1956. Same musicians as: "Between The Devil And The Deep Blue Sea."

This is absolutely amazing jazz music. In fact, I have saved the best for last. I have heard a lot of jazz in my life, but this piece, "Night in Tunisia," by the very "straight" foursome known as The Modern Jazz Quartet, is by far and away the best that I have ever heard. Thank God these guys never let heroin addiction compromise their seemingly flawless musicianship when this was miraculously created in the summer of 1956. Milt Jackson is simply sensational on vibes.

PLAYLIST #9
"BEST OF 1970"

IT WASN'T DIFFICULT for me to pick one year from my remote past for this particular playlist theme. 1970 has to be the year for me, not only for my personal life (I turned 18, and graduated from high school), but also it was the year when music became a huge part of my life, and has been ever since.

It was in 1970 that Dennis F and I started our first band together, Rockwater Buck. Oh, to have a time machine so that I could go back, just for one glorious day, and relive being young and carefree again, and jamming as a hormonal-raging teenager. Life was so sweet at age 18. I had the phone numbers for 3 different chicks. All I had to do was get on the phone and call one of them, and she would be available for some heavy make out sessions in the dark. It was fabulous. And I used to always eat those Pillsbury Chocolate Energy Sticks that the Apollo astronauts ate while traveling to the moon. I was absolutely addicted to them.

I can also recall Nixon in the White House trying to end the war in Vietnam with "honor" and I was appalled at what happened at Kent State in May. My favorite TV program, when I watched it, which was seldom, was "Then Came Bronson," about a biker dude who traveled the country, much like Peter Fonda and Dennis Hopper in my favorite film that year, "Easy Rider."

I got my first car in 1970, a candy apple red 1967 VW bug, and I can recall filling it up for a buck and a quarter, before going out to Whittier

MIND TAVERN

BLVD and cruise, with Dennis F riding shotgun. But best of all, my parents were relatively young and alive; I would give up 10 years of my future life just to talk to them again. The songs that I have included on my list today represent my favorites from all the "new stuff" I was listening to back then. KNAC FM was the radio station I listened to while doing my homework during my senior year at Whittier High, and it was on that progressive station that I heard some of the greatest rock music my ears had ever heard. And now, I would like to share some of those very cool sounds. On with the music...

1. Moody Blues, "Never Thought I'd Live To Be A Hundred," "Beyond." (4.00)
Recorded in 1969, from the album, *To Our Children's Children's Children* I heard this one on the KNAC in January of 1970, and thought it was very cool. When I heard it again later, I recorded it on cassette because my radio was also a cassette recorder. I played this piece over and over again until the tape died. I like its dream-like quality; an otherworldly feel. And the two pieces transition well, forming a single musical experience. Indeed this is a great band from the good old days.

2. Grand Funk Railroad, "In Need" recorded in 1969, from the album, *Grand Funk* (4:30)
I absolutely dug this hard rock, garage band in 1970. Backed by Mel Schacher on Bass and Don Brewer on Drums, Mark Farner, in my opinion, was simply the best "raunch rock" guitarist in the business at that time. He could whip up the huge crowds of kids who would go to the big stadiums to see him rock out. But was he a "Hendrix?" No, not even close. But I thoroughly enjoyed Farner's wah-wah technique, his interesting guitar riffs, the sound of his Gibson as he wailed on it, and even his vocal delivery. This piece was my favorite from their second album.

3. Johnny Winter, "Memory Pain" recorded in 1969, from the album, *Second Winter* (4:30)
Again, I first heard Johnny Winter on the KNAC. In fact it was this piece that I'm sharing today. When I first listened to this rollicking blues piece, I was amazed at Winter's clean, crisp playing style, and I loved his speed. Winter was definitely one of the fastest of all the Rock guitar heroes during that time. I knew Hendrix was amazingly fast, but this guy Winter truly captivated me in 1970. So much so, that I did my Senior English research paper that spring on "Johnny Winter." Grade? C+

4. Cream, "Deserted Cities of the Heart," recorded in 1968, from the album, *Wheels of Fire* (3:38)
That winter I was into Cream. I would spend hours in my Hoover Street pad, playing Wheels of Fire, Disraeli Gears, and the Live album, all of which I played full blast on my stereo. Rock legend Eric Clapton is backed up by two excellent musicians, Jack Bruce and Ginger Baker. This piece is my favorite "Studio" recording of the power trio.

5. Jimi Hendrix, "Message To Love" recorded December 31, 1969, at the Fillmore East, New York, from the album, *Band of Gypsies* (5:22)
Here's the "King" of Rock guitarists. Jimi Hendrix was simply second to none. He changed guitar playing into something completely different and newly amazing in the late 60's. His genius was in the way he could produce a myriad of different sounds from his electric guitar, which he played left-handed. I chose "Message To Love" from my favorite rock album of 1970, *Band of Gypsies*. Hendrix just wails on this one. Billy Cox is on Bass, and Buddy Miles on drums and backing vocal.

6. The Beatles, "Get Back" recorded in 1969, from the album, *Let It Be* (approx. 3:00)
This was my favorite from the "Let It Be" album that came out in May. I can recall Dennis F coming to my Hoover Street pad one evening, wearing

a brand new pair of blue jeans from Jean's West, and carrying a newly purchased copy of this great album, bought at American Records. Both stores, which were favorites of ours, had just opened up in Uptown Whittier that spring, and we both thought this album was the Fab Four's best. Later that summer we saw the movie version, and of course the best part of the film is when the band plays this song live on the roof of Apple Studios—a great song indeed.

7. Crosby Stills Nash and Young, "Woodstock" recorded in 1970, from the album, *Déjà vu* (3:53)

KNAC FM radio was a major discovery for me in 1970. Up until that year, I only listened to station KRLA, and the Top 10. But with this more powerful, clearer sounding FM station, Rock music became much more real and alive. Woodstock by CSNY was definitely my favorite by this band. It came out in April, around Spring Break, and I first heard it on KNAC, and recorded it. This brings back memories of going to Huntington with Dennis F and his brother on Easter weekend, and meeting blond chicks by the pier.

8. Led Zeppelin, "Bring It On Home," recorded in 1969, from the album, *Led Zeppelin II* (4:20)

Dave B, lead guitarist of Rockwater Buck, was the one who first told me about English guitarist, Jimmy Page. He said that Page was even faster than Hendrix. So I went to Lovell's record store in Uptown, and got their first two albums. This piece is a full bore, rock blues masterpiece from their second album. Robert Plant's vocal and harmonica playing are beautifully integrated into this piece. John Bonham provides a solid bottom on drums and John Paul Jones plays a great bass.

9. Blind Faith, "Presence Of The Lord," recorded in 1969, from their only album (4:50)

I first read about this off-shoot band of the Cream in Newsweek Magazine during the summer of 1969. And since Eric Clapton and Ginger Baker were teamed up with rock prodigy, Stevie Winwood, I was very interested in their first album, which unfortunately was their only album. I chose to play this particular piece because I think it is Clapton's best work on guitar. In my opinion, the whole album is a minor masterpiece.

10. The Band, "We Can Talk," recorded 1968 from the album, *Music From Big Pink* **(3:00)**
During spring break I went to Hinshaws department store. I bought a new suit for my upcoming graduation from high school, and an LP by a band called, The Band. I first heard about this great group from Steve B, and he recommended this particular album—Music From Big Pink. I immediately liked it. I was quite impressed with The Band's technical tightness and over-all country-rock sound. But it is a different kind of country rock, one without cowboys. This piece is my favorite from that classic 1968 LP.

11. Savoy Brown "Savoy Brown Boogie," recorded in 1969, from the album, *"A Step Further."*
I first heard this hard-rocking band in concert, in September of 1970, at the old Santa Monica Civic Auditorium, and loved their performance, especially The Boogie. Later I bought this album at Lovell's, and Dennis F and I would play it constantly at my Hoover Street pad. This is definitely one of the best boogies I have ever heard, before or since.

PLAYLIST #10
"MY BEST EMOTIONAL FRIENDS IN 2005"

AS MY GOOD FRIEND, DAVE B, put it so profoundly back in 1970: "Music is life." And that quote has been so patently true down through the years of my life. Certain pieces can represent milestones or benchmarks as we travel the "road of life," buttressing our emotional ups and downs.

This particular year has been no exception for me. So today, I would like to share those pieces that have been my "best emotional friends" during this darkest of my 53 years on this planet. My musical recollection goes back to the first of the year in January, when I was obsessed with Bob Dylan's great early albums. So I have chosen to play some of his amazing music from the mid 60's. Then as the winter progressed, my dad moved in with us for the last month of his life. During that awful time, as I watched my dad slowly die, my interests moved to some of the early 1950's pop sounds of the Hit Parade. So I have included a smattering of some of the great music of Nat King Cole, because my dad liked him so much when I was a kid.

Also during the final weeks of the winter, I watched the fascinating film, The Virgin Suicides. So I have included the main piece from that film's very ambient soundtrack by a group called Air. There is one more piece from this depressing time of my life that will forever stand out in my mind, the piece that I was playing downstairs in my office at perhaps the precise moment my father passed away, directly above me in Kathryn's bedroom (about 10:30 PM on March 3) – Gentle Giant's

"Peel The Paint." (Even though my father's official date of death is Friday, March 4, both Sue and I feel he probably passed on the night before, right after Sue tucked him in at 10 PM).

After my father's funeral in March, I bought the DVD film bio of Ray Charles, and after watching that film a couple times, I went through a two month listening odyssey of Ray Charles music— mainly his early 60's pieces with chorus and orchestrations. So I have included two great masterworks by the "blind genius."

When spring break came in April, I thought a lot about the people I have known in my life who are now deceased, like Dirk J for example, and so I purchased Dirk's favorite Tom Waits LP – Small Change, from 1976. I have included one piece from that collection on this playlist. As the summer began, I got into the music of Russian composer Serge Prokofiev and his very styled, Lt. Kije Suite. For this list, I included one movement from this work. Then I sailed into the luxurious sounds of Brahms and his first piano concerto. For this list, I offer the Adagio movement from that masterpiece. When Labor Day came, I spent the weekend watching Monterey Pop. The last act, Ravi Shankar, is simply stunning. As the school year began I wanted to explore some new progressive rock groups. So may I introduce to my fellow music fans two personal discoveries, the progressive rock sounds of Dream Theater and Porcupine Tree. Now for the official list:

1. **Bob Dylan, "Pledging My Time" (3:42)**
2. **Bob Dylan, "Most Likely You Go Your Way And I'll Go Mine" (3:22) from Blonde On Blonde, 1965**

What can I say about this great artist that hasn't already been said by literally hundreds of writers and critics and fans. Blonde On Blonde, in my opinion, is by far his Magnum Opus; nothing, not even Highway 61, comes close to this amazing double album. I chose two pieces from this collection to play today, because they are timeless classics that I personally never grow tired of hearing. Great lyrics and Dylan's inimitable singing style make for some fantastic listening. These are my two all-time favorite Dylan pieces.

3. Ray Charles, "Ruby" 1960 (3:00)
4. Ray Charles, "You Don't Know Me" 1962 (3:00)
As a kid growing up in suburban Whittier back in the early 60's, I recall hearing Ray Charles music on KRLA regularly. The two pieces I have chosen for today are my two favorites — from the times when the Dodgers were the best in the National league; when Kennedy's Camelot was still alive; when a gallon of gasoline cost only 15 cents, or less if there was a gas war going on; when this country was not at war with anyone and when there weren't terrorist assholes plaguing the world with their zealous insanity. Indeed, great days that are long gone. Sit back and let these two pieces cleanse your soul with their cool, kickback melodies of a time when "relative innocence" was the way of the world.

5. Nat "King" Cole, "Mona Lisa" 1950 (3:00)
6. Nat "King" Cole, "Too Young" 1951 (2:30)
My dad had two favorite musical artists whom he enjoyed hearing all throughout his long lifetime: Marty Robbins and Nat Cole. This playlist includes two classics by the smooth and suave artist known as "The King". It was truly a shame Cole had to die so young, too young, in fact, back in 1965 at age 46. So now, I play these two masterpieces of early 50's pop music for my dad, who I am sure, is in heaven listening to both Marty and Nat, putting the heavenly choirs to shame.

7. Tom Waits, "Step Right Up" 1976 from *Small Change* (5:39)
Dirk J one day said to me: "Hey dude, you gotta hear this new Tom Waits album." So he put it on. The one piece that really stood out inside my mind was "Step Right Up." Great poetry and outrageous sax playing! Dirk was so inspired by this piece, he penned his own lyrics in the Tom Waits style: "Close To Flight." It was this piece that Dirk prophesied his

own premature demise. Again, way too young— "too many whiskies… too many nights… some strange by-pass gland goes, and I'm thrown into flight."

8. Air, " Playground Love," from *Virgin Suicides* soundtrack 2000 (2:30).

Talk about cool jazzy sax playing. This piece is as cool as it gets. Virgin Suicides is one movie that always leaves question marks in one's brain after watching it. How is it possible that 80 teens a day in this country commit suicide and no one seems to be doing anything about it? (Do the math — that's about 30,000 a year) I play this piece for them—the forgotten dead.

9. Gentle Giant, "Peel The Paint," from *Three Friends* 1972 (5:00)

I knew it was about to happen… I played this early 70's, prog rock song late in the evening of March 3, and the subtle, footsteps-like beginning of this interesting Gentle Giant piece reminded me of death incarnate, tip-toeing quietly and unobtrusively up the stairs to Kathryn's room, where my dying father lay, waiting patiently with hands folded in prayer, and stole his soul home.

10. Porcupine Tree, "Dead Wing" (5:00) 2005

When I play this band, I can hear a little bit of Police, a little bit of The Who and a lot of King Crimson. The beginning to this 2005 progressive rock piece is deceptively subtle, but it doesn't take long for these guys to start rocking. The guitar work is solid and tight. I also enjoy the drumming on this one.

11. Dream Theater, "The Root of All Evil," from *Octavarium* (8:07) 2005

I like these guys. As with Aphex Twin, they grow on you after a while. I wanted to explore and share some new stuff for this listening playlist, so I went on Amazon and read numerous Lists by satisfied consumers and collectors, and found this band along with Porcupine Tree on many lists, so here is my favorite from this very interesting CD.

AND NOW FOR SOME CLASSICAL PIECES:

12. *Lt. Kije Suite* **(Op. 60), Serge Prokofiev (18:00) composed in 1933**
This is a very satisfying rendering by the London Symphony Orchestra with Sir Neville Marriner conducting. According to the liner notes of the CD, this music was composed for a Russian film that was never made. No problem with me as the listener. This is simply great program music – 20th Century style. All 5 movements are wonderfully nuanced but the highlight in my opinion is the last movement which is the burial of Lt. Kije. It is easy to enjoy this great music.

13. *Piano Concerto #1 D Minor* **(Op. 15), Johannes Brahms, "Adagio," (14:00) composed in 1854.**
Initially this greatest of all piano concerti was supposed to be a full-fledged symphony. But the Maestro changed his mind when his inner circle of artists and musicians basically told him he was not mature enough to compose a complete symphony, so he converted it to a concerto of sublime proportions. Most of the ideas for this magnum opus came about when Brahms was in his early 20's. This adagio movement, played sensitively by the greatest of all the Romantic virtuoso pianists – Rudolf Serkin, still brings goose bumps to my back when listening to it. Serkin is beautifully backed up by conductor George Szell and the Cleveland Orchestra.

14. Ravi Shankar "*Raga Bhimpatasi***" Video recorded at the Monterey Pop Festival – June, 1967 (18:00)**
I end this playlist with one of the most electrifying musical performances I have ever seen on video. It is almost on par with Joe Cocker's tour de force at Woodstock. Simply put, this is Indian Sitar music at its best.

And the tabla playing (the bongos) isn't too shabby either. This music simply takes off and flies. As you watch, notice the expressions of some of the "blown away" audience members who were there that day… Mike Bloomfield, Jimi Hendrix, et al. Astonished by Shankar's unworldly virtuosity, these young hippies (now old enough to be grandparents) had never heard anything like it before, and they obviously loved it. This classic video clip, from the 1968 film, Monterey Pop, by American filmmaker, D. A. Pennebaker, is highly recommended, and can be seen on YouTube.

PLAYLIST #11
"VIDEO MUSICAL MASTERPIECES"

THIS PARTICULAR PLAYLIST was so much fun to research. I decided to go eclectic and include some progressive rock, jazz, German techno, the avant-garde, American classical and a little bit of Stravinsky! As I was researching music for this project, I discovered that in order to fully experience and appreciate the musical moment, and get a full taste of the live performances offered on the DVD, it is essential to play at least 12 to 15 minutes of it. So my individual recommendations are in that time frame. So without further ado, I submit for your approval this collection of some truly amazing video performances of musical magic. As far as I can tell, most of these recordings can be seen on Youtube. Otherwise, they are on DVD for a price.

1. King Crimson – *Eyes Wide Open* – "Dangerous Curves" and "Lark's Tongues In Aspic, Part IV" Recorded April 16, 2003. Live in Tokyo, Japan. Robert Fripp, Trey Gunn, Pat Mastelotto, Adrian Belew (15:00)

Crimson still beckons me and continues to delight. I found this DVD on Amazon and decided to give it a try. I was not disappointed. This is an amazing concert by Fripp and Company. "Dangerous Curves" includes some spacey sounds, reminding me of some of Crimson's older albums of the 70's; it then builds up to a high point like Fracture, which interestingly leads into the rocking "Lark's Tongues." As you watch, notice Fripp rocking out in the dark, out of the spotlight. This is great progressive rock music, indeed.

2. Peter Gabriel, – *Growing Up Live* – "Here Comes the Flood," "Darkness" – Recorded May, 2003 – (12:00)

Watching Peter Gabriel play "Here Comes the Flood" takes me back in time, way back to 1979, when I first heard the piece at Dennis F's pad. I can still see us as young men, hanging out and jamming—Jeff K, Dirk J, Cal-Boy, The Dude—we were all at a cross roads in our lives, with marriage looming for everyone. This is extremely enjoyable concert footage to watch; it is obvious Gabriel is still in top form. I especially like the subtle tonal nuances of "Darkness."

3. Kraftwerk, – *Minimum-Maximum* "Autobahn" and "The Model" (13:00)

I first heard about this interesting German group back in the early 90's, when I heard "Autobahn" on the radio. These guys offer a different concert experience, in that they essentially stand still playing their respective instruments. But they do manage to produce many surprises nonetheless. The background images during the pieces add a lot to the overall concert experience, and the music itself is hypnotic and very catchy. With "Autobahn," I can imagine cruising at high speed down the autobahn highway in Germany, taking in the sights in my fast-moving sports car. A very cool piece indeed.

4. The Keith Jarrett Trio – *Live at Open Theater East* – July 1993 "Butch and Butch" (7:24)

Now I offer the very cool jazz of Keith Jarrett with this interesting jam session going on between Jarrett, Guy Peacock and Jack DeJohnette. Jarrett gets in to it during this piece, displaying some truly great jazz virtuosity. Technically, he is indeed an accomplished musician. But I must be honest and say that I do not appreciate his loud groaning and grunting while playing. It was most annoying. However his overall playing overshadows the annoyance.

5. Harry Partch – Enclosure 8 – "*Castor and Pollux*" performed by Ensemble Partch. Recorded in 2006 (17:18)
It may take considerable time to acquire a taste for Harry Partch music. But once this is accomplished, one is in store for hours of fascinating listening. I have actually grown to enjoy the twangy discourse emanating from his invented instruments. "Castor and Pollus" is a 17 minute dance piece with energetic dancers in costume integrating the musical performance. For this piece, Partch calls for 6 dancers and 7 players, and together they created this interesting foray into the avant-garde.

6. Alexis Weissenberg performs *Petrushka* (3 movements) composed by Stravinsky. Filmed in Stockholm, January, 1965. Directed by Ake Falck (15:00)
Here is a great example of amazing piano artistry mixing with highly creative film-making to produce an unforgettable concert experience. Alexis is simply brilliant as he fingers the keyboard in ways both astonishing and miraculous. Imagine the amount of time needed to rehearse and ultimately master this remarkably complex piece. All 3 movements are enthralling to hear and to watch, but the finale is unbelievable.

7. George Gershwin – *Rhapsody in Blue* 1924 performed by Berliner Philharmoniker, Seiji Ozawa- conductor; with the Marcus Roberts Trio – Marcus Roberts- piano; Roland Green- Bass and Jason Marsalis- Drums. Recorded Live at the Waldbuhne, Berlin, June 28, 2003. (21:00)
When I first watched this version of Gershwin's Magnum Opus, I wondered what George would say if he could somehow come back from the dead to see this concert, with a very cool and adept jazz trio playing along with a full orchestra, in performing his greatest piece. I'm sure he would have been impressed with the energy, technical bravado and the aesthetic drive of Marcus Roberts, the blind keyboardist of the trio. This is amazing concert footage at its best.

8. Aaron Copland, *Appalachian Spring,* **1945 San Francisco Symphony Orchestra, Michael Tilson Thomas- conductor. (25:00)**
I have had a life-long relationship with Copland's remarkable Appalachian Spring. I can recall sitting in the bleak darkness of my Hoover Street bedroom, back in the early 70's, being depressed over female relationships, and finding great solace in listening to this fascinating music. This exquisite unabridged version is the original score, calling for 13 musicians only, with the piano adding so much to this particular performance.

PLAYLIST #12
"MUSIC FOR SOLO PIANO AND NEW YORK, NEW YORK!"

PART ONE — THE SOLO PIANO

FOR THIS PLAYLIST I decided to concentrate on solo music, centering on my favorite instrument: The Piano. I have always had an affinity with the keys going back to when I was 9 years old. I can recall pounding the black and white ivories with clueless delight at Patty M's house in 1961 in the midst of her 9th birthday party.

Although I never had formal training, (nor am I a "concrete" pianist with any discernible talent), I basically approached playing the instrument in an organic manner…completely spontaneous. Even though most of my recorded output is junk, I am nevertheless proud of the "junk" I have created on recorded tape.

As for my library of commercial LP's, cassettes and CD's, my favorites dealing with solo piano are herein listed below, gleaned with tender soulful care, after 60 plus years of listening and collecting.

1. Chabrier, "Idyll" from *Dix Pieces Pittoresques* 1880 (3:20)
My all-time favorite composer of piano music, Maurice Ravel, claimed in his last essay: "Recollections Of My Lazy Childhood" (written in 1937 while he was going mad) that one Emmanuel Chabrier, and not Debussy, was his utmost inspiration and influence. He stated: "I did fall under the spell of one musician: Chabrier. Not yet has he been given the rank that he deserves, for modern French music all stems from him…" This being so, I

sought out the piano works of Chabrier to find out for myself what Ravel was talking about. I purchased the Erato CD with all his works played sensitively and commandingly by Pierre Barbizet. This particular selection is my favorite. The music soars emotionally like a bird in flight, wavering here and there, then triumphantly finding a place of rest. Delightful.

2. Ravel, "Oiseaux Tristes," from *Miroirs* 1905 (3:33)
Ravel, in writing about this piece, stated: "…In it I evoke birds lost in the torpor of a somber forest during the most torrid hours of summer." Personally, I see the mind of a superb composer unraveling to the inevitable collapse of mental illness. This music is amazingly played by Abbey Simon from the Vox Box collection.

3. Ravel, "La Vallee des Cloches," from *Miroirs* 1905 (5:56)
Gorgeous impressionistic music here…subtle, sedate, almost resigned. No one, in my opinion, comes close to Ravel in putting together such intensely emotional piano music; music straight from the heart. Again played with virtuosity by Abbey Simon.

4. Debussy, ""Des pas sur la neige," from *Preludes* Book I (4:14) composed in 1909
My personal favorite of the Preludes by Debussy. I first heard this piece via the electronic sound of Tomita in 1974. It is so low-key and distant. Imagine sloshing through the snow on a high mountain top somewhere far away from the insanity of modern life. About this set of Preludes, Debussy wrote: "Don't listen to the advice of anyone but the wind, which tells us the history of the world as it passes." Peter Frankl is the interpreter here, recorded on Le Box from Pantheon.

5. Tchaikovsky, "Berceuse," from *18 Piano Pieces* Op.72, (3:38) composed in 1893
This delightful, inspiring piece, written in the last year of his life, is my

favorite of all of Tchaikovsky's body of solo piano works. Its rocking, atmospheric quality evokes feelings of long ago days spent with by-gone personages. I think of my mother a lot when I play this and I tend to play it often in the fall. This is another Vox Box recording, rendered masterfully by Michael Ponti.

6. Mendelssohn, "Allegretto con espressione," from *Sonata for Piano, Op. 6* (5:56) composed in 1826.

Written when Mendelssohn was only 17, it is obvious he had Beethoven in mind. A critic of the time described the lyricism of his piano works: "His fingers sing!" This, the first movement, is cast in sonata-rondo form in 6/8 time. I love it for its simplicity and passion. This recording is from Columbia with Murry Perahia at the keys.

7. Beethoven, "Adagio Sostenuto," *Sonata No. 14 in C-Sharp Minor,* (Op.27, No. 2), 'The Moonlight" (6:54) Composed in 1801.

This is perhaps the best from The Maestro— Ludwig Van Beethoven. Here we have the tones of the piano sounding like a solemn prayer to God. Some critics might call this piece cliche and hackneyed, but I still am in awe of it. I recall hearing this for the first time at Rio Hondo College in the fall of 1970. Marilyn R was my Sunday afternoon date and we held hands through the entire performance. This performance is by Philippe Entremont from the Columbia LP entitled The World's Favorite Piano Music.

8. Chopin, "Polonaise Fantaisie," Op. 61 (13:05) composed in 1846.

This stirring rendition is played by perhaps the greatest of all Chopin interpreters: Vladimir Horowitz. This recording is a Live performance at Carnegie Hall in April of 1966. As for this piece, Franz Liszt described it as being "marked with feverish and restless anxiety" and found that "a deep sadness, broken constantly by startled movements, by sudden alarms, by disturbed rest reigns throughout."

9. Chopin, "Etude In E," Op. 10, No. 3, (3:33) Composed in 1830.
Definitely one of my all-time favorite solo piano pieces. I first heard this one back in 1965 while watching the "Million Dollar Movie" on Channel 9 in LA. That particular week during the fall, they were showing and reshowing "The Golden Age Of Comedy," a documentary about the comedy silents of the 1920's. After each segment, this piece was played by an orchestra, and I grew to like its somewhat melancholy tone. I generally enjoy all of Chopin's etudes, especially the one created for "black keys" only. But this one is still the best.

10. Grieg, "Wedding Day at Troldhaugen," from *Lyric Pieces*, Op. 65 (5:08) Composed in 1896.
Being a big fan of Grieg's A Minor Concerto for Piano and Orchestra, I decided to invest some money in an entire collection of his solo piano music. I was not disappointed. In this VOX Box CD collection, there is over 3 hours of interesting music, most of which are entitled "Lyric Pieces." My favorite is this one. It has an engaging, compelling strut to it that I find emotionally satisfying.

11. Rachmaninoff, "Prelude in C Sharp Minor," Op. 3, No.2 (4.32) Composed in 1892.
I end this playlist with this very dramatic, almost bombastic, piece by the Russian genius, Rachmaninoff. I love the way this one builds up to an apex of hope; then descends to the nadir of despair. I cannot erase from my mind the vision of Marilyn Monroe whenever I hear this composer's music. He was the ultra Neo-romanticist.

PART TWO — NEW YORK, NEW YORK!

I can well recall my one and only journey to the Big Apple back in the summer of 1968. Aside from being paranoid by the throngs of people walking in the streets, I can vividly recall the stupendous views from the

Empire State Building as it swayed in the wind. All those taxi cabs from up there looked like little yellow bugs. And the elevator ride up to that airy perch seemed to take forever. I can recall climbing up the musty spiral staircase to the crown of the Statue Of Liberty, and perusing the blue Atlantic through dirty panes of glass. It is indeed an amazing city with a rich history of fantastic music. It has, after all, Carnegie Hall and Broadway— the mecca for the stage show and musical. Like Paris of old, New York has been, and still is, the mecca for art in this country. I decided to theme the second part of this playlist around the music of New York, New York! As you can see, the chief Guru of New York musical art is none other than Leonard Bernstein, the Maestro of the New York Philharmonic back in the late 50's until the 60's. When I hear this music, I can feel the bustle and the urbane sophistication of that unique town.

1. Bernstein, "Opening: "New York, New York," from *On The Town* (11:27) recorded in 1958.
Outstandingly vibrant music here. I love the opening baritone voice as a new day begins for 3 sailors on leave in New York City. Bernstein's rollicking tones are dynamic and unforgettable.

2. Bernstein, "Dance: Times Square," from *On The Town*, 1958 (4:00)
I first heard this piece back in the 1970's, when I purchased Columbia's Greatest Hits LP for Bernstein. Again, I love his jazzy, classical fusion of sounds.

3. Bernstein, "Fancy Free Ballet" 1963 (Approx. 10:00)
Another great composition by Bernstein. The piano is bluesy, snappy and then very low-key, and I can visualize a jazz cafe in Herald Square or thereabouts, with bright neon lights flashing, and girls drunk on booze, posturing for dates. Great "New York" music here.

4. Gershwin, "Andante con moto" from *Piano Concerto in F* (12:24) composed in 1925.
This is my favorite movement from Gershwin's masterpiece concerto for piano. The urbane jazzy feel to it is so palpable. This is even better than Rhapsody In Blue in my opinion.

5. Copland, "*Billy The Kid*," (Movements 2, 3 and 4) (approx. 10:00) composed in 1938. New York Philharmonic Orchestra conducted with verve by Leonard Bernstein.
I include this masterpiece by Aaron Copland because he wrote it with New York audiences in mind. Its modernist sound is sophisticated and inspiring, even though the music is about a social outlaw from the Old West. I can play it over and over again and never grow tired of it.

6. Bernstein, "Prelude, Fugue and Riffs for Solo Clarinet and Jazz Ensemble," Benny Goodman on clarinet, recorded in 1963 (7:00).
Outrageous jazz by Bernstein again. And what a treat to have Benny Goodman play clarinet for this one. Definitely one of my all-time favorite New York style jazz pieces.

7. Modern Jazz Quartet, "Delauney's Delimma," (3:54); date of recording unknown.
I purchased this LP back in the early 70's. When you think of pure jazz, the cities of New Orleans, St. Louis and Chicago come to mind. But with the Modern Jazz Quartet, it's New York: I marvel at the deliberate preciseness of this group and I love Milt Jackson's Vibes.

8. Bernstein, "Dance: The Real Coney Island," from *On The Town*, 1958 (approx. 5:00)
This is just plain psycho-music with some satirical musical barbs thrown at our Arab "friends." Frenetic and suave at the same time, I end this playlist with the concluding number from *On The Town*.

PLAYLIST #13
"PLAY THESE BEFORE YOU DIE"

1. Rhapsody In Blue (Gershwin – 1924)
I've heard several versions of this 1920's masterpiece, fusing Jazz and classical elements. But the Leonard Bernstein rendition with him at the piano is, in my humble opinion, the best. Bernstein's "Bluesy" style at the keyboard and the fact that he is in no hurry as he performs the cadenza, makes this recording absolutely transcendent.

2. Tuba Concerto in F Minor, 2nd Movement – "Romanza, Andante" (Vaughn Williams -1954)
A delightful short piece that exudes a majesty of sounds, but at the same time is profoundly humble. Never has the tuba sounded better. I discovered this one back in the late 80's, and I still consider it a musical serendipity.

3. Violin Concerto in D, Op.35, 3rd Movement, "Finale, Allegro," (Tchaikovsky- 1878)
Most aficionados of the genre of Violin Concerti will pick the Mendelssohn Concerto in E Minor as the best of the genre, and I agree it is a wonderful listening experience; however, for sheer emotions in music, this 3rd movement of the D concerto alone makes Tchaikovsky the "KIng" of Violin Concerti. The notes of this nearly impossible-to-perform concerto run the gamut from frolicking insouciance to the nadir of emotional despair.

4. Symphony #9 in D Minor (Choral) last movement, (Beethoven- ca. 1824)

Set to Schiller's "Ode To Joy," this is the Mt. Everest," the apex, of all symphonic literature. If the listener is not moved to spiritual ebullience while listening to this tour de force, something is definitely amiss. A piece imbued with the brotherhood and freedom of mankind.

5. Symphony #8, last movement, (Mahler – 1906)

If Beethoven had lived another 30 years, he would've probably written symphonies like Mahler's. The last movement of the 8th (the Symphony of a Thousand) is absolutely apocalyptic in scope. A total listening rush.

6. Symphony #6 "Pathetique" 4th Movement (P. Tchaikovsky – 1893)

Tchaikovsky's "Death" symphony. The last movement is a riveting musical statement, dripping in tragedy and pathos. It is a suicidal plunge into the fateful darkness. This was the first symphony I get hooked on back in the 60's.

7. Excursions for Piano, Op. 20 (S. Barber – 1944)

Perhaps my favorite piano work by an American artist; this piece borrows from classically American idioms and folk tunes, producing something even the maestro George Gershwin himself would probably envy. I recall first hearing this at Cal-State Fullerton with Dennis F back in 1975.

8. Nocturnes (Satie – 1919)

What can I say? Except Satie's music changed my life. The Nocturnes, in my opinion, are his best. This music takes you very far away, and it conjures up a thousand memories of past youthful days during the 70's.

9. Le Deluge op. 45 (Saint- Saens – 1875)
Replete with Biblical overtones, this moody piece is the epitome of post-Romantic French tone poems. The violin soars like an eagle; its highs and lows producing a passion that is quite palpable. "Lobster Tail" for the ear.

10. Appalachian Spring (Copland – 1944)
I end this playlist with my all-time favorite "classical" piece. Suffice it to say, if I had to go to a deserted island for 6 months and I could take only one classical piece, this would be it. A "12" on the my scale of "10".

PLAYLIST #14
"WE ARE THE MUSIC MAKERS; WE ARE THE DREAMERS OF DREAMS"

1. Aphex Twin, "We Are The Music Makers," (7:42) from *Selected Ambient Works 85-92*
The more I hear the fascinating music of Richard D. James, the more I like it. All his stuff is quite infectious, and like a fast-growing vine,, it grows on you after awhile. I particularly like the bass lines on this piece. Minimalist and very interesting.

2. The Tatum Group, "Plaid," Recorded September, 1955 (6:38) Art Tatum- Piano; Lionel Hampton- Vibes; Harry Edison- Trumpet; Buddy Rich- Drums; Red Callender- Bass; Barney Kessel- Guitar
This is some of the best jazz music I have ever heard. Lionel Hampton's vibes playing in this piece is simply superb.

3. "I Wonder Who," *The Live Adventures Of Mike Bloomfield And Al Kooper*, recorded September, 1968 (6:02) Al Kooper- Organ; Mike Bloomfield- Guitar, Vocal.
I can recall seeing Mike Bloomfield at the Golden Bear in Huntington Beach back in 1971; in fact I wrote a small chapter about that concert in Jamming in Suburbia. He was definitely one of the best blues guitarists around back in the late 60's with The Electric Flag. I can also recall listening to Bloomfield jam on the piano that night before the concert began, and he was even better on the piano playing the blues than the guitar, and

that is indeed saying something. Sublime late 60's blues music here by one of the "Masters."

4. "Midnight Rambler," Rolling Stones from *Get Yer Ya Yas Out*, recorded November, 1969 in New York City. (7:00)

I first heard Midnight Rambler in October, 1970 at Chris B's house when the Floro Brothers played it. Then I received this LP for Christmas in 1970 and was immediately hooked by this great rock n' roll classic by the "greatest" rock n' roll band of all time. Keith Richards' guitar is mesmerizing. I think I have played this piece at least a thousand times in my lifetime.

5. "Don't Let it Bring You Down," Annie Lennox, from *Medusa* – recorded in 1995 (3:36)

I became a big Annie Lennox fan when I saw American Beauty in 2000. This particular piece can be heard in the background during the scene when the Kevin Spacey character seduces Mena Suvari. A great cover of a great Neil Young opus. I know this is a bold statement but, I think Annie does a better job with this song than Neil himself. I know…I know… bold.

6. "Con Te Partiro," composed by F. Sartori and L. Quarantotto, sung by Andrea Bocelli from Romanza (4:09) recorded in 1995.

Remember those interesting Bellagio casino ads on TV back in the mid-90's? When I first heard the voice of the blind opera singer, Bocelli, I was totally impressed. I have since bought two cd's by this gifted vocalist. Such control…such range. Even better than Caruso or Mario Lanza.

7. "Smoke On The Water," Deep Purple from *Live In Japan*, recorded in 1972 (7:27)

Again, thanks to the Floro Brothers, I first heard Smoke On The Water in

1974 at Whittier High School, when Jeff, Jerry, Jeff M and Greg B ("the Bert Reynolds of the band" as Jeff announced that day) did an excellent rendering of this hard rock masterpiece. This CD was recorded in Japan in 1972 when this great band was at its peak. This kicks ass.

8. "The Lark Ascending," composed 1914 by Vaughan Williams (14:15) recorded in 1986 by the Royal Philharmonic Orchestra; Andre Previn conducting.
I guess I should retitle this playlist: "Music Introduced To Me By Jeff F"— For it was he who told me about this marvelous masterpiece by Vaughn Williams at a friend's wedding in 1987. Listen to the gorgeous violin as it glides and soars and descends gracefully like a lark. An absolutely lovely piece of music.

9. "Baia," music video from Disney's *The Three Caballeros* (5:00) 1945 composed by Ary Barroso and Ray Gilbert
This interesting music video selection comes from the Disney masterpiece of animation, The Three Caballeros. If ever a musical selection conjures up a dreamscape, this is it…the epitome! Aesthetically speaking, the song is indeed quite beautiful and exotic, and the animation that goes with it, of beautiful Baia in Brazil, is breath-taking. Notice the amazing colors of the calm waters, the old churches, the jungle and the mountains. An absolutely gorgeous and ingenious integration of sounds and sights.

10. "Trouble Every Day," The Mothers Of Invention; composed and sung by Frank Zappa; From *Freak Out* (1966) (5:19)
I end this playlist with this highly charged piece by Mr. Zappa. No doubt this was written in reaction to the 1965 Watts Riots. The lead guitar (by Zappa) is great, and the other 'mothers' provide a very solid backing, especially the cool harmonica playing. I'm sure Bob Dylan was also a big influence behind this one. Listen for Frank's matter-of-fact statement in the

middle of this song: "Hey, you know something people. I'm not black, but there's a whole lot of times I wish I could say I'm not white." Pretty bold words for its time. A true genius.

PLAYLIST #15
"BRIAN ENO (AND TWO FRIENDS)"

FIRST LET ME SAY that the following pieces by Brian Eno do not include anything from two of my all-time favorite albums – *No Pussyfooting*, with Robert Fripp, and *Thursday Afternoon*. Those two great albums are a bit long. But let it be known—They both belong on this playlist of the best in ambient music by Brian Eno.

1. "Lizard Point" (4:34) 1978 From *Ambient 4 – On Land*
One of Eno's more fluid ambient pieces. I first heard this back in 1995 and I was completely blown away. Listening to this is like being sucked into some deep vat of the sweetest honey imaginable.

2. "Lantern Marsh" (5:33) 1978 From *Ambient 4 – On Land*
This is one of Eno's best "industrial" ambient pieces in my opinion. This sounds like something right out of David Lynch's Eraserhead – a veritable industrial nightmare. A piece filled with inhuman cries and hopeless wails. A very fitting piece for the times in which we currently live.

3. "Unfamiliar Wind" (Leeks Hills) (5:23) 1978 From *Ambient 4 – On Land*
Just close your eyes when listening to this… and be there. When I listen to this one, I see myself as a tiny human being, riding on the head of a bee as it soars and flies through a fragrant but sweltering meadow. A total escape from all my daily travails.

4. "M386" (2:50) 1978 From *Music For Films*
A totally flipped out quasi-rock piece from the lowest echelons and bowels of Eno's deep sub-conscious. It's extremely hard for me to explain why I like this piece so much except that when I first heard it, I had never heard anything like it before.

5. "Failing Light" (4:17) 1980 From *The Plateaux of Mirror* With Harold Budd
An absolutely gorgeous piano piece with some very heavenly harmonies, giving off a feeling of one's last moments of life on Earth. I play this piece in honor of all those poor souls who ended up in tiny pieces after the World Trade Towers came crashing down. A very sad, low-key and hypnotic piece.

6. "Late October" (4:38) 1984 From *The Pearl* With Harold Budd
This piece and Lost In The Humming Air are my two favorites from this very cool CD. Again, Eno and Budd do an amazing job of collaborating. Imagine a forlorn, late October afternoon, alone in the fields with your thoughts and memories of fading youth.

7. "Lost in The Humming Air" (4:19) 1984 From *The Pearl* With Harold Budd
I consider this piece to be the closest thing to Thursday Afternoon, but obviously a much shorter version. Very fluid and dynamic, this piece is perfect for meditation or reading poetry. A very relaxing and spiritually edifying piece.

8. "2/1" (8:25) 1978 From *Music For Airports*
I love the "voice-choir" sound effect in this one. I assume the voices have been realized on a synthesizer or a mellotron. A very soothing and enriching musical experience.

9. "Ikebukuro" (16:05) 1985 From *Shutov Assembly*

I'm convinced that this piece has the power to actually heal one's emotional wounds. It is imperative one partakes before taking in this masterpiece of ambient sounds. A very therapeutic, intensely spiritual piece that is better than sex, or a back message. Well, on second thought, maybe sex is better still… you decide. You need to relax and close your eyes. Let it flow through you.

10. "Evening Star" (7:48) 1975 From *Evening Star* With Robert Fripp

The most beautiful guitar work Maestro Fripp has ever done, in my opinion. An absolutely great piece that leaves a plethora of goose bumps. Time for a complete musical catharsis.

11. "An Index Of Metals" (28:36) 1975 From *Evening Star* With Robert Fripp

I realize this is a long one, but the whole piece has to be experienced in order to truly benefit from its vast treasure trove of sounds. Its ultra- rich musical layers seem to stand still as you listen, but it is, nevertheless, an extremely dynamic piece that transforms and reinvents itself in a miraculous way. Perhaps and debatably so, this is Eno and Fripp's finest musical moment together.

PLAYLIST #16
"23 OF MY FAVORITE 45'S FROM THE 1950'S"

FOR THIS PLAYLIST, I would like to recommend 45 minutes worth of musical memories, with 23 of my favorite 45's from my early childhood during the seemingly carefree decade of the 1950's.

I was five years old when I received my very first 45 record platter. It was a tune by Marty Robbins entitled "A WHITE SPORT COAT." I can recall being absolutely enthralled by the sounds of his down-to-earth voice and his twangy guitar. After that, more records would follow—records by Elvis Presley, The Big Bopper, Little Richard, Ricky Nelson, David Seville, Jodie Sands, Eddie Fontaine, and many others, and before long (since these disks only cost 50 cents a piece at the old Model Market) my collection burgeoned.

Most of my fondest childhood memories center on the music of that time. My older brother also collected 45's during that seminal time, and I credit him as my primary influence. I remember spending hours inside his small bedroom on Mavis Street, playing my 45 records on his very cool 45 record player.

One of my favorite pastimes as a child was pretending that I was a disc jockey on a make-believe radio station, like KFWB, Channel 98, and I'd introduce each tune to my fantasy radio audience, like the guys I listened to all the time while growing up: Bill Balance, Art Laboe, Dick Biondi, Emperor Hudson, Bob Eubanks and Dave Hull. So here are my favorites from long ago:

MIND TAVERN

1. "A White Sport Coat," Marty Robbins (2:00) 1957
I was in Kindergarten when this was a popular tune on the radio. I spent my carefree days riding my scooter and collecting and trading baseball cards. Steve Bilko, the home run hitting superstar of the Angels, was every kid's idol during those days before the Dodgers came west from Brooklyn. The Mickey Mouse Club was on every afternoon and I never missed it, or Mouseketeer Karen's dimply smile.

2. "Gotta Get To Your House," David Seville (1:32) 1957
This piece is a typical example of the humorous, novelty songs readily available for sale at the Model Market back in the late 50's. The entire neighborhood where I grew up visited the Model Market at least 3 times a week. The butcher was named Elmer and he wore thick black glasses. And he was always carrying around a huge meat cleaver, and there were bloodstains always on his white butcher's coat.

3. "Come Go With Me," The Dell Vikings (2:10) 1957
I remember hearing this piece on KFWB constantly when I was 5 years old. My dad would take my brother and me to the pier at Newport once a month back in 1957- 1959, and we'd fish off that old wooden pier until the wee hours of the morning, listening to a transistor radio. I can still hear this Dell Vikings classic out there on that pier, so very long ago.

4. "So You Think You Got Troubles," Marvin Rainwater (2:00) 1957
My dad liked those faddish, humorous novelty tunes as much as my brother and I did, and he recommended Marvin Rainwater to us. Here is two minutes of "down home" humor.

5. "I'm Walkin,'" Ricky Nelson (1:56) 1957
Ricky was just a pimply teenager when his dad, Ozzie, casually suggested that his youngest son sing a song on the "Ozzie and Harriet Show." It was

a brilliant idea, and practically overnight, a new rock n' roll teen idol was born. The rest, as they say, is rock history.

6. "With All My Heart," Jodie Sands (2:47) 1958

When Jodie Sands recorded this pop song, I was a 6-year-old first grader at St. Mary's School, trying to figure out how to read and write. Sister Evangela was my teacher that year, and I can recall being loudly ridiculed in front of the class by that nun for not being able to draw a straight line with my pencil. So, I started hating her and school, "with all my heart."

7. "Keep A Knockin," Little Richard (2:10) 1957

Little Richard was amazingly popular in 1957, along with Elvis, Fats Domino, Jerry Lee Lewis and Chuck Berry. This piece was my favorite during the summer of '57, as well as all the other kids on Mavis Street. We all thought his piano playing was "keen" and his singing style even better than Elvis.' But according to my brother, the priests and nuns at St Mary's disapproved of Little Richard's (sexual) energy, as well as the John Birch Society, at least according to Dennis N's mother, Mary, a staunch Catholic and John Bircher. "Turn that music off! It is music for Communists!! Turn it off!!"

8. "Planet Rock," Royal Teens (2:04) 1958

This is the flip side of the main piece: "Short Shorts." Women in 1958 were beginning to wear "short shorts" during that long ago summer, showing more leg flesh than ever before. Hence this novelty record by a group called the Royal Teens. After I grew tired of "Short Shorts," I decided to play Side B, and discovered that I liked it much better. I must have played this record a thousand times during the waning years of the 50's and unfortunately, this record is cracked. And has been for over 40 years.

9. "Beep Beep," The Playmates (2:20) 1958

For awhile in 1958 every kid on my block wanted this silly novelty tune because the speeding car doing all the "beeping" in the piece is a little Nash Rambler, and everyone knew that the Nash was a tiny little car, even smaller that the VW bug. If anything, this was a "one hit wonder" for the Playmates, based on the "tortoise and the hare" story.

10. "Nothin' Shakin'," Eddie Fontaine (2:06) 1958
One day in Kindergarten, when this piece was hot on KFWB, I was the only boy who wanted to play "house." I figured if I chose "House" that day instead of "art" or "blocks," the very cute Nancy S would pick "house" too, since that was her favorite choice all the time. And then, I surmised, we could play together in total ecstasy, alone in that little place! But alas, she surprisingly didn't pick "house" that day, and there I was, the only kid inside that stupid, sissy playhouse. Obviously, there was 'nothing shakin' that day, as far as my current female "crush" was concerned.

11. "Big Bopper's Wedding," Big Bopper (2:07) 1958
Another novelty tune by the popular Texan DJ, The Big Bopper. We all know this legendary figure was on the same plane in 1959, along with Buddy Holly and Richie Valens, when "the music died." There is some nice saxophone playing on this piece.

12. "Young Love," Tab Hunter (2:04) 1958
Tab Hunter "scored" in the mid 50's when he starred in the Warner Brothers' musical, "Damn Yankees." Then, like a host of other male teen heartthrobs of that time, starting with James Dean, Tab had his 15 minutes of fame— with this paean to teen romantic love.

13. "Teddy Bear," Elvis Presley (2:03) 1957
In 1957 I lived in a little white house on Mavis Street in the suburbs of LA. But at age 5, I thought it was huge. Every day the Good Humor Man drove down the street in his white ice cream truck with his starched white cap atop his head. Across the street lived Mr. Gumm who delivered

Hostess cupcakes to stores in his big white truck. Everyone on my street was white, along with the newly cemented sidewalks. Elvis Presley was a white man who sang black man's music, and popular rock n' roll was born. Where are you, King Elvis? The ghosts of Mavis Street are beckoning you to gyrate once again.

14. "Street Of Memories," Johnny Ray (2.00) 1957
Johnny Ray was known for mussing his hair and singing so emotionally, that it seemed he was on the verge of a complete breakdown, which of course made all the girls scream. He wasn't Elvis or Sinatra even, but for a time he was the "cat's meow." My mother bought this record for me in 1957, and I think I know why. But I never heard her scream.

15. "Diana" Paul Anka (2:29) 1957
Paul Anka wrote this tune when he was only 15 years old, and it was his first big hit. He also wrote the music for the Tonight Show, starring Johnny Carson, and it made him a fortune.

16. "The Purple People Eater Meets The Witch Doctor," Joe South (2:35) 1958
Another silly novelty tune. But I loved it back in 1958. In the spring of that year, all the kids flew kites on Mavis Street. The sky was literally filled with them, and usually they would get tangled together or in the tall Elm trees that provided shade in the summer. My brother crashed his red devil kite in our front yard Elm tree that spring, and I recall it stayed there for months, stuck hopelessly in the twigs of the branches. As I listen to this long ago song, I can still see that kite, struggling with the wind to free itself.

17. "Mr. Sandman," The Chordettes (2:00) 1957
This is definitely one of my all-time favorites from the 1950's. And I believe it was a million seller for the Chordettes. I wonder whose voice it was that said, "Yes" when the girls intone: "Mr. Sandman?" A recording

engineer? A boyfriend of one of the girls? Who knows? I bought this one at the old El Mercado shopping plaza on Beverly and Norwalk Boulevards with my brother. "You're buying that?" he asked quite stunned. "Yes," I replied, a bit surprised. "That's for sissies," he said. But I didn't care.

18. "Wake Up Little Susie," Everly Brothers (2:00) 1957

A great piece by the Everly's. This was the second 45 record I acquired, only because my brother didn't like this song. He was an avid collector of 45's like myself and he usually bought all the great songs before me, because, after all, he was 5 years older than I, and had more money. He used to be a paperboy for the LA Mirror newspaper, and he'd play his 45's loudly when we folded all those papers before he delivered them on his Schwinn bike with the gooseneck handlebars.

19. "The Chipmunk Song," The Chipmunks (2:17) 1959

If you were a normal, average American boy in the 1950's, you probably had this 45 record of speeded up voices, depicting 3 chipmunks singing in harmony. Silly? Maybe, but it was popular during a time when life was sane and secure. Give me the Chipmunks any day. It's better than the music of today in my opinion.

20. "Hound Dog," Elvis Presley (2:00) 1956

Both my brother and I wanted this record badly when it first came out in 1956, but my dad said we had to wait and that only one of us could buy it. We were not allowed to have two copies of the same song in the same house, even though the record only cost 50 cents. So, we had to flip for it during the spring of 1957, there at the Record Hut, right next door to the old Wardman Theater on Greenleaf Avenue. Guess who won?

21. "Tom Dooley," Kingston Trio (3:01) 1959

In 1959 this was a big hit for the Kingston Trio. I recall feeling odd listening to it because poor Tom would soon be dead, hanging from a willow tree. Whenever I felt odd, especially about death, I would go out and play with my little matchbox toys on the driveway. It was nirvana for a 7-year-old boy with freckles on his face.

22. "I'm Gonna Sit Right Down And Write Myself A Letter," Billy Williams (2:05) 1957
In 1957 while playing this record among many others inside my brother's small bedroom on Mavis Street, we'd build model airplanes with sticky smelly glue that would dry up on our fingers quite quickly. Revell models were only 59 cents at the Model Market, and the planes we liked to build were World War 2 types. My brother would play this piece over and over again because it was a catchy tune that we never grew tired of. The long title was catchy too.

23. "Cocoanut Woman," Harry Belafonte (3:15) 1957
I end this 1950's playlist with this Harry Belafonte classic. Latin sounds were all the rage in the 50's with bongo and conga drums dominating. I close my eyes as I listen to this piece and inside my mind I see a 5-year-old boy sitting in the shade under a tall elm tree. He is alone, and he is waiting with his free stick for the ice cream man, and life is good.

PLAYLIST #17
"WENDY'S LIST AND PERSONAL FAVORITES FROM THE PAST"

FOR THIS PLAYLIST, I have included carefully picked samples from the 1950's record collection of a teenage female by the name of Wendy Reniers. (Her name appears handwritten on numerous labels of the 45's). My dad picked this collection up at a garage sale for probably a buck somewhere in Whittier back in the 1970's.

The brown carrying case is still in excellent condition, with its plastic handle beckoning thoughts and reveries concerning the hand that once owned this box back in the 50's, what type of girl was Wendy? What did she look like? Is she alive now? If so, she would be a woman in her 70's. The evidence of said female can obviously be seen in the meticulously kept records, handwritten in a looping cursive style. And since the ink changes in her listing as her collection grows, I can see maturation in her writing and musical tastes as well.

I figure Wendy was about age 15 when she first began compiling this modest collection in 1956, the year of her first listing: "Singing the Blues" with Guy Mitchell. Overall, her choice of artists? Very eclectic and reflective of the conservatism of that mid 50's, Cold War time; Eddie Fisher, Jim Lowe, Sonny James, Perry Como and Guy Mitchell. We have healthy doses of the Everly Brothers, Gale Storm, Billy Williams, Pat Boone and Ricky Nelson as well.

But it's not about who's on Wendy's List of great mid-1950's pop music, it is who she left off... The King himself, Elvis Presley. Not one 45 by Presley is in the "Wendy Collection." And I find that strange. Perhaps, being Catholic, Elvis, being frowned upon by nuns and Pope Pius the 12th, was an artist Wendy was reluctant to buy. Or perhaps because of a parental edict of some kind, Wendy dared not to even think about buying an Elvis 45, or it meant a serious grounding. Or it could be surmised Wendy simply didn't like Presley's liberal, hormonal style, since her overall tastes in music is conservative and not too far from the beaten path, unlike Elvis.

Nevertheless the absence of Presley from such a well-thought out collection remains baffling. As for the records themselves, all seem to be in pristine shape after 60 years. I can tell they were at one time treasured and tenderly cared for by the girl named Wendy. After studying Wendy's notes, and allowing 2:30 minutes per song, I decided to pick 25 from her listed collection of 50. The 25 chosen were selected with great care, thought and respect for the spirit of "Wendy Reniers."

PART 1 – WENDY'S LIST

1. "Cindy, Oh Cindy," Eddie Fisher
2. "Green Door," Jim Lowe
3. "Tonight You Belong To Me," Patience & Prudence
4. "Hot Diggity," Perry Como
5. "A Sweet Old Fashioned Girl," Teresa Brewer
6. "He," Al Hibbler
7. "After School," Randy Starr
8. "Warm Up To Me Baby," Jimmy Bowen
9. "Party Doll," Buddy Knox
10. "Why Baby Why," Pat Boone
11. "A Teenager's Romance," Ricky Nelson
12. "Gone," Ferlin Husky
13. "Love Me To Pieces," Jill Corey
14. "Knee Deep In The Blues," Bruce Adams
15. "Dark Moon," Gale Storm
16. "Date With The Blues," Billy Williams

17. "Lucky Lips," Dottie Evans
18. "Somebody Up There Likes Me," Jack Daniels
19. "Bon Voyage," Janice Harper
20. "Lips Of Wine," Andy Williams
21. "Tell Me That You Love Me," Paul Anka
22. "Cross Over," Jimmy Bowen
23. "Hi-Ho Stevo-O Louis Nye
24. "Got A Date With An Angel," Billy Williams
25. "Rebel," Carol Jarvis

PART 2 – PERSONAL FAVORITES

1. "Spill The Wine," War (1970) approx. 3:00
Ah yes…1970…when life was so deliciously free and easy. Cruising the Blvd and sun tanning… those memories come back to me when I hear this great song from the Summer of '70. I have always enjoyed the work of Eric Burden. His music has a boozy, slinging in the shade quality about it, and I can still see myself driving "The Red Ball Jet" on Whittier Blvd, summer of '70, playing "Spilled The Wine" with Dennis F riding shotgun.

2. Aphex Twin (1994) approx. 5:00
Some of the most spaced out ambient music I've heard, eclipsing Brian Eno himself in terms of its unique layering with a variety of interesting, meshing sounds. I love the beat in this, and its contagious off-centeredness. Highly recommended CD.

3. "Killing in The Name," Rage Against The Machine (1992) (approx. 4:00)
Outrageous LA hard rock from the early 90's. The guitar is sensational; some of the best I've heard since Hendrix. The Hip-Hop styling and the profanity at the end do not bother me too much mainly because the hard

rock is so awesome and compelling. Prepare to be swept away by the sheer power of this excellent hard rock outfit.

4. "Toccata And Fugue in D Minor," J.S. Bach, 1704-1708, played by E. Power Biggs, (8:25)

It is impossible to have a playlist book without J.S. Bach. He is indeed the "Father Of Music." This is his greatest piece by far—a veritable whirlwind of organ sounds that are still musically transcendent. Close your eyes and see visions of pure blissful heaven. As one listens to this monumental cascade of organ sounds, one can appreciate the depth and width of Bach's furious genius.

5. "Interview," Gentle Giant (1976) (6:54)

Dennis F turned me on to Gentle Giant in 1974. This is from their great LP from summer, 1976. "Interview" pretty much epitomizes the exuberant sound of this mid 70's Prog-Rock band. DF was living on Broadway in the back house, summer of '76 was waning, and we'd sit in his house and play Gentle Giant. Great piece from a great time. I am still completely amazed at the superb technical skills of these guys.

6."The Knife," Genesis (1971) from *Trespass* (8:55)

I've been exploring Genesis lately during my drives in the Moving Stereo System, the Explorer. Genesis still has a hold on me if you will, and more than just for nostalgia. It is just plain good music…interesting, dynamic, progressive… without too much bombast—this is Genesis at the beginning, 1971. Dennis F used to play this at his Bright Street apartment back in 1974, and we'd party, ending the night eating lots of ice cream. I tend to think this is the best piece on Trespass.

7. "War In Heaven," William Bolcom (1974) (13:18)

Dennis F turned me on to the music of William Bolcom back in 1974 with his midnight playings of the Nonsuch recording of "The Black Host." DF was living over in the Bright Street apartments and we'd listen to music in his bedroom, filled to the gills with strawberries. We found this recording at the Wherehouse in 1975. "War In Heaven" is a great avant-garde piece, bringing forth both beautiful and coarse layers of sounds. The piano in this is sublime, even in its raunchiest moments. It has some "guts" to it. This is one of my all-time favorites.

8. "Reverie," Claude Debussy (performed by Tomita, 1973) (4:45)
Ahhh yes…Tomita and his gorgeous renditions of Debussy. Again, Dennis F turned me on to this album in 1974. All of the pieces are superbly realized, utilizing an array of electronic keyboard sounds. This one is my favorite.

9. "In C," Terry Riley (composed in 1964) recorded in 2002 by the European Music Project.
I end this playlist with Terry Riley's tour de force of modern minimalism— In C. I first heard this piece in the spring of 1973 in my Music of Today class at Cal State Fullerton. I recall the professor not saying a word on the first day of class. Instead he put this recording on the record player in the classroom and played the whole thing full blast for half an hour. Like Fripp and Eno's "Index of Metals," this piece seems to stay in one spot, but is extremely dynamic at the same time.

PLAYLIST #18
"LIVE VIDEO PERFORMANCES FROM ED SULLIVAN, WOODSTOCK AND THE FILLMORE"

FOR THIS UNIQUE PLAYLIST, I decided to look for video clips that had a "historical" perspective with regard to the first 25 years of the Rock n' Roll era. In doing so, I was amazed at just how spoiled we were back in the 50's and the 60's. Compared to today's sterile, hard-edge, decadent, diva-type sound, our generation indeed had it good, as these particular video examples will attest.

PART 1 – ED SULLIVAN SHOW CLIPS

It was religion. Watching the Ed Sullivan Show every Sunday night at 8 p.m. back in the 50's, 60's and early 70's was tantamount to going to Mass for all Americans, including the "Baby Boomers" who invariably spent their allowances on records.

In my novel, In-A-Gadda-Da-Vida, I described that amazing Sunday night in 1964 when the Beatles made their American debut. How could anyone alive that night forget it? It was indeed electric, and absolutely life-changing.

I can even recall seeing Elvis back in 1956 when I was 4 years old. I knew then that this guy from Memphis was exciting, someone great to listen to, and to be honest, he was the one responsible for turning me on to Rock n' Roll music for life.

I guess one could say that the Ed Sullivan Show was the platform, the conduit, the jumping off point, for all the great musical artists during the first 3 decades of rock history. Without Ed Sullivan, these artists were basically not going to succeed in the pop music business, or be heard by the record-buying public.

I have included some great groups in these clips from television history. There are approximately 25 minutes of Ed Sullivan excerpts which can be seen on Youtube.

And as Ed would always say at the beginning of the evening: "Tonight, we have a really really big shew for you!"

Elvis Presley (1956) "Hound Dog"
Buddy Holly and the Crickets (1957) "Peggy Sue"
Beatles (1964) "I Want To Hold Your Hand"
Beach Boys (1964) "I Get Around"
Rolling Stones (1966) "Paint It Black"
Animals (1966) "Don't Bring Me Down"
The Doors (1967) "Light My Fire"
Steppenwolf (1968) "Born To Be Wild"
Chambers Brothers (1968) "Time Has Come Today"
Creedence Clearwater Revival (1969) "Proud Mary"
Sly and the Family Stone (1968) "Dance To The Music"
Martha and the Vandellas (1965) "Dancing In The Streets"

PART 2 – GREAT ROCK FESTIVALS / CONCERTS OF THE 60'S AND EARLY 70'S

Janis Joplin and Big Brother & The Holding Company, "Ball And Chain" (5:45) *Live at the Monterey Pop Festival* **– 1967**
A "female Joe Cocker," Janis Joplin throttled her listeners with a singing style that reflected her problem-laden childhood in Texas. Not exactly Barbra Streisand or Julie Andrews, this rock diva from the mid 60's nevertheless evoked strong emotions from those of us who appreciated her rough-hewn vocal approach. This excerpt from D.A. Pennebaker's film,

Monterey Pop Festival is a bit heart-rinding, knowing full well she didn't have 5 years to live. But what a talent! Raw talent, yes, but real talent. There hasn't been anyone like her since.

Richie Havens, "Handsome Johnny" (5:00) *Live at the Woodstock – 1969 Film Clip produced by Bob Maurice and Michael Wadleigh, 1970*
Joe Cocker's performance at Woodstock was astoundingly great. I think we can all agree to that statement. But I have already included that clip in another playlist. So, not wanting to leave Woodstock off this particular list, I have included my second favorite act – Richie Havens' superb performance of "Handsome Johnny." I recall seeing this film in Hollywood with my friends in June of 1970, and when I saw Havens jamming with such a contagious zeal, I couldn't believe he was making all that great music basically by himself with only an acoustic guitar. This is simply a tremendous performance.

John Lennon and the Plastic Ono Band, "Yer Blues" and "Don't Worry Kyoto (Mummy's Only Looking For Her Hand In The Snow)" (10:00) *Live at the Toronto Peace Festival – 1969*
In 1970 on those unforgettable Friday nights when Rockwater Buck jammed in the basement of my Hoover Street pad, we would take tea breaks upstairs in my bedroom. And while sipping our cups of tea, I would play the Live Peace album with John Lennon and Eric Clapton on guitars, and a screeching Yoko on backing vocal. As I recall, we couldn't believe that Apple Records would actually publish some of the "shit" on this LP, especially Yoko's screeching songs. But with time and a lot of maturity on my part, I have changed my mind about this album. Now I consider it vanguard, avant-garde rock, and quite interesting to hear and to see. I've included two pieces today: "Yer Blues" with some excellent guitar by Clapton, and "Don't Worry" by Yoko with some very cool guitar static accompanying her. Film clips produced by D.A. Pennebaker.

Jimi Hendrix and the *Band of Gypsies*, "Who Knows," (9:32) Live at the Fillmore East, New York, December 1969.
What an amazing artist. I first heard *Band of Gypsies* during Spring Break in 1970 on KNAC FM radio. I was chewing on some Pillsbury Energy Sticks when this song – "Who Knows" came on, and I loved it immediately. Although Buddy Miles is a tad bit clumsy on the drums, and Billy Cox holds his own on Bass, it is Jimi's playing that propels this piece from trite mediocrity to classic greatness.

The Who, "My Generation," and "Magic Bus" (12:00) Live at the Isle of Wight – 1970.
According to the Guinness Book of World Records, The Who takes top honors for being the loudest rock band of all time. And this clip of two of their top songs at the Isle of Wight in 1970 proves this fact. I was never much into The Who back in the mid 60's, but when I saw them on the Woodstock movie, I was totally blown away by them. Then when I bought the "Live At Leeds" album, that pretty much sealed things for me. They are essential for any playlist of classic rockers.

Joe Cocker & Mad Dogs and Englishmen, "Delta Lady" and "Feelin' Alright," (10:00) Live in at the Fillmore East, 1970.
Steve B, now a musical "legend" himself, albeit on the listening side of the spectrum, drove me out to Hollywood in his Skylark back in 1971 to see this film of Joe Cocker and the Mad Dogs. We were both suitably impressed by the excellent music and of course Cocker's spirited singing. We were equally impressed with the Master of Time and Space – Leon Russell, and his excellent keyboard and guitar playing. My favorite song is "Space Captain" but I wanted to include two pieces back to back, so I've chosen "Delta Lady" and "Feelin' Alright." Actually all the songs are great, and nostalgically fun to watch and hear.

PART 3 – 1970'S PROGRESSIVE ROCK

Gentle Giant, "Features from Octopus" (13:00) Live at the Terrace Theatre, Long Beach, California, 1975.
I end this video playlist with the virtuosity of Gentle Giant at the height of their playing-in-concert powers. In this clip we see the various band members display their musicianship on multiple instruments, playing various songs from their album, "Octopus." Dennis F turned me on to this group back in 1974, and I can recall being immediately struck in a positive way by their amazing range and technical prowess. I also saw these guys at the Whiskey in the fall of '74, and was completely blown away. I'd like to buy the complete works of this top-flight progressive rock group, only if the price is right.

PLAYLIST #19
"MUSIC I'VE BEEN LISTENING TO LATELY"

HEREWITH IS MY PLAYLIST #19. This deluxe menu of sounds contains some interestingly rendered euphonic experiences, that I have specially chosen. There is no theme really for my choices. Except to say, I have been playing these pieces quite often. Artists include Bela Bartok, Michael Jackson, David Clayton Thomas, Eric Burdon, Kurt Cobain, Hank Williams, Chris Squire and Trevor Horn, and a group I had not heard about until 2009 by the name of Spacemen 3.

1. Bela Bartok, String Quartet #2 (1st Movement) (10:12) composed 1915-1917 Performed by the Hungarian String Quartet
My favorite Bartok opus, even better than his short "Piano Pieces." This is some serious stuff though. And not simple at all. This particular movement requires more than sheer virtuosity to perform, but an immense musical soul. This piece conjures up visions of The Holocaust for me. It is hauntingly creepy at times, yet resolute and unyielding. When I listen to this moody melancholy masterpiece, I visualize the Hungarian Jews being rounded up by Nazi black shirts, and the resulting heartbreak from families and homes being destroyed by racism. Music needs to be more than silly escapism, but a document without words that says so much about good and evil and the overall paradox of trying to survive in a world where we have so little control concerning events and attitudes.

2. Nirvana "The Man Who Sold The World," from Unplugged in New York. 1993 (3:30)

Kurt Cobain was an idiot, let's face it. He married a dippy blond gold digger and he took way too many drugs. And to top that, he was stupid to kill himself so early in a very promising musical career. But his music is endlessly interesting to hear. This piece was performed Live on MTV back in 1993, just before the shotgun blast. Like all his stuff, it grows on you. Nice guitar work and an engaging piece that doesn't destroy the ear drums.

3. Michael Jackson, "The Way You Make Me Feel," 1987 From Bad (5:00)

For so many years I ignored Michael Jackson music, considering it pop music crap not worthy of my attention or dollars. But since his death, I decided to open my musical mind and give Michael Jackson a chance. And so, I bought Thriller and Bad and listened to his music all summer as I drove around in my car. By late July, I had discovered Jackson's music to be quite interesting, if not entertaining, and I actually liked several of his songs, especially from the Bad album, which I think is far better than his classic best seller – Thriller. This piece, in my humble opinion, is his best one. It has a nice solid bass line, and I like Michael's over-dubbing vocals throughout. You have to admit it, this piece moves and it's difficult not to tap your feet.

4. Blood, Sweat & Tears, "And When I Die," 1968 (4:00)

I've been experiencing a "BST" mania lately, mainly for nostalgic reasons, since 1968 was a comparatively simpler time for me. David Clayton Thomas' distinctive voicing style makes this piece, along with some fine harmonica playing. I can recall spending quiet evenings in 1969 in front of the fireplace in my folk's old home on Hoover Street with my 17year old girlfriend, listening to BST in the glowing darkness. I had no job, no bills to pay, nothing but freedom to be young and to simply spend romantic moments with my girlfriend. Life was indeed good.

5. Spacemen 3, "Come Down Easy," from The Perfect Prescription 1987 (6:46)
I discovered Spacemen 3 after reading through Amazon's Listomania. Many people there were raving about them so I decided to give this group and this highly recommended LP a try. After one listening, I was immediately hooked. This is the most interesting song from the album, along with "Transparent Radiation." This particular piece has a rollicking, boogie-like beat and it reminds me so much of our own music from the old days of the 70's. All of this band's music, in fact, is unique, somewhat deranged, very spiritual and intense, and always interesting to listen to.

6. The Animals, "Monterey" 1968 (4:37)
The Animals' catalogue is replete with great memorable songs, including this one about the Monterey Pop Festival of 1967. The Sitar effect is quite interesting in this, and, of course, the nostalgic roll call of past rock icons by vocalist Burdon, gives this piece a haunted quality, as if these artists are emerging from the dead to play again. Again, to be young again in 1968. That would be something.

7. Hank Williams, "Why Don't You Love Me" 1950 (2:22)
The best country-Western, Honky- Tonk song by The Master – Hank Williams. The steel guitar adds so much to this piece, and, of course, it pretty much epitomizes Williams' classic musical style. Most of Hank's pieces bespeak of tough times with broads and booze, and it's a shame he burned out so early in 1953. No one compares to him— before or since.

8. Yes, "Leave It" 1984 (3:30)
I first heard this Yes piece back in 1984 and I recall enjoying the harmonic, over-dubbed vocals of Chris Squire and Trevor Horn. Dennis F turned me on to this excellent progressive rock group back in the early 70's as we made our nightly journey to Coco's. "The Dude" invariably played his 8-Track collection of the early albums, especially the Fragile album. Later

MIND TAVERN

I heard the virtuosity of keyboardist Rick Wakeman and then I realized this was a group worth investing in. I'm sure we all have our particular favorites from Yes, and this one is mine.

9. Spacemen 3, "Transparent Radiation," from The Perfect Prescription 1987 (9:00)
I end this playlist with one more interesting piece by Spacemen 3, my favorite new "Find" from this past year. I am impressed with their simple, down-home approach with their musical ideas. They are not trying to be superstars here; just 3 guys having fun, jamming. This piece includes some really nice violin playing along with the guitar work. As I stated, their music grows on you, and you find yourself playing their stuff over and over again. I highly recommend The Perfect Prescription to all music fans.

PLAYLIST #20
"A TRIP TO LOVELL'S RECORD STORE"

MY FIRST TRIP TO LOVELL'S record store in uptown Whittier, if my memory serves me correctly, occurred in early 1964, at the height of Beatlemania. Back when "She Loves You" hit Number One on the charts, and I decided to buy the 50 cent single, Lovell's was mostly an electronic appliance store, selling Hi Fi record players, TV's and radios. And located in the back of the store, beyond the furniture-like phonograph systems and new color TV's, were the records.

There were the expensive LP's hanging on display on pegboards, artists like Ray Charles, Andy Williams, Wayne Newton and Dean Martin. But what most of us adolescents were interested in were the size 45 singles of the hottest songs played on KRLA radio. And in was in the back of the store where all of the store's customers congregated, going through all those 50 cent singles. What was so odd about Lovell's was that the fact three quarters of the floor space were devoted to the big TV's and the bulky Hi- Fi systems, and it was empty of customers most of the time.

Later on, Lovell's got the hint and decided to opt out of the stereo/TV business and concentrate on records and cassettes only. And that change saved them from bankruptcy, at least according to my dad, who was their CPA for years. I first met Tom, the owner of Lovell's, in 1971. He was this cool dude who worked the cash register all the time, and he hired cool guys to cover for him when he was in the back doing paper work. For years I made regular trips to Lovell's to buy a record. And there Tom would be, at his usual spot behind the counter, ringing up my $3.00

record album. I would say that my busiest buying time was between 1970 and 1974, buying classical and rock LP records on a weekly basis. Who knows how much money I spent there, but I would reckon in the high hundreds of dollars.

Basically my theme for this playlist is a throwback to the years of 1972 and 1973, when I was in college and basically buying LP's of both rock and classical music at Lovell's. This playlist includes a mixture of rock and classical; pieces I played quite often back when all I had to worry about was keeping my grades up, staying out of the draft, and keeping a girlfriend. Life was an amazing roller coaster of emotional highs and lows, of insecurities and stupid jealousies, of busy times and idle times, of endless trips to college and to Lovell's, and all this music represents those crazy days in the early 70's—a time when I was just beginning my manhood.

1. Canned Heat, "Woodstock Boogie," Live at Woodstock, 1969. (12:55) from Woodstock II

I remember the legendary Steve B was the first on our block to get this album at Lovell's. And I believe the year was 1971. I didn't get my copy until 1973 and I can recall wearing out the grooves of the record. I haven't heard this version of the Boogie in years mainly because I never bought the CD of this excellent compilation. I just know the boys rocked out that night in August of '69. I must have played this recording a hundred times in my little back room on Hoover Street. I never grew tired of it.

2. Alexander Borodin, "Dances of the Polovtsi" and "Nocturne Promenade" (7:45) Music composed in 1887-1890. Camarata / Kingsway Symphony Orchestra. Album released in 1970.

Borodin epitomized late 19th Century Nationalism with his gorgeous evocations to old Russian folk songs, ever prevalent in his music. His best, most well-received pieces, would have to be his Polovtsian Dances and his Prince Igor opera. Borodin did a number on my head back when I was

21. His stuff made me horny all the time so I can recall romancing my girl a lot while playing this beautiful music. I found this rare LP at Lovell's in 1973, priced at 4 dollars.

3. Buffalo Springfield, "Pretty Girl Why" (2:24), "Special Care" (3:30), "Uno Mundo" (2: 00). (7:54 total time)

I bought the Greatest Hits album, a two record set, in early 1974 at Lovell's, and then of course played all of their hit songs a hundred times in a row. Then I discovered 3 pieces on Side 4 and I realized I like them better than "Bluebird," or "Rock N' Roll Woman." And those pieces are classics. It has been decades since I last heard these 3 very interesting pieces by Stephen Stills and company.

4. Bela Bartok, Piano Concerto No. 3 for Piano and Orchestra, Movement Two, "Religioso" (10:39). Composed in 1945. Philippe Entremont, piano; New York Philharmonic, Leonard Bernstein, conductor.

In 1972 I was at Lovell's and saw this album of Bartok music. I was intrigued because it was a Bernstein album so I decided to take a chance on it. It blew me away completely. I would stay up late at nights, open up the windows of the back room on Hoover Street and play this masterpiece movement very loudly. It is perfect night music, and I haven't heard it since 1972 at least. This was Bartok's last piece before dying; in fact, he didn't quite finish the last few remaining bars of notes in the last movement. His son and a student filled in the appropriate notes after Bartok's death in 1945.

5. John Lee Hooker and Canned Heat, "Whiskey and Wimmen" (4:33) Recorded April, 1970. Album released in 1971.

I dug the boogie blues sound of Canned Heat for most of 1971. I saw this album at Lovell's featuring John Lee Hooker and decided to give it a try. I immediately liked the combination of the two factions: Old versus

The New. I can recall digging "Whiskey and Wimmen" the most with its hard-driving boogie sound.

6. Georges Bizet, "L'Arlesienne " Suite No.1, 1872 (15:37) Philadelphia Orchestra, Eugene Ormandy conducting.
This is some of the best music in all of the classical genre. I bought the Bizet Greatest Hits album at Lovell's one day in 1972 mainly because I was bored with the latest composer I had learned about at school. So I took a gamble on the composer of Carmen, and this French opera master was a great find indeed. I discovered his music to be perfect for studying and reading. I must have played the "L'Arlesienne Suite" a hundred times during the year of 1971 alone. Masterful orchestrations in this music.

7. Johnny Winter, "Tribute To Muddy," (6:20) from The Progressive Blues Experiment; recorded live at the Vulcan Gas Company, Austin, Texas; circa 1968.
I recall buying this LP at American Records in Uptown during the summer of 1970. At the time I firmly thought Johnny Winter was the best guitarist in the business; so even though the album looked and smelled like it was a cheap bootleg, from Imperial Records no less, I decided to give this album a try. I think I paid $1.98 for it (much cheaper than Lovell's) and surprisingly I found out there were some excellently-played, hot-sounding jams on this record. I picked "Tribute To Muddy" because it was the one title I remember.

8. Joaquín Rodrigo, "Adagio" Concierto de Aranjuez for Guitar and Orchestra, composed in 1939 (9:56) Philadelphia Orchestra, Eugene Ormandy. John Williams- Guitar. From the Greatest Hits / The Guitar Album, published by Columbia, 1972.
The classical record section at Lovell's was most impressive. Tom, the manager, always kept this section well-stocked, even though Rock albums

were obviously his "bread and butter" items back in the early 70's. To his credit Tom stocked the store with classical records for the "layperson" so to speak. In other words, albums for the hippies who were learning about this genre in college and were becoming interested in its universe of sound riches for the first time. Columbia Records evidently sniffed out this new market and came out with its "Greatest Hits" series of interesting LP's, each centering on a particular composer. And so, I bought the whole set at $2.98 a piece over a 2 year period. The last one I bought was this tribute to classical guitar. I can vividly recall making out with my big-bosomed girlfriend while playing this exquisite music in the dark. I haven't heard it in decades.

9. Jethro Tull, "Inside," from Benefit, 1970, (4:00)
Now here is an obscure song from the very obscure album Benefit by Jethro Tull. Again, in was the summer of 1970 when I picked up this disappointing LP at Lovell's. I had heard one of their songs on KNAC FM radio that spring and liked it, and I thought maybe that song was on this newer album, and I thought wrong of course. The only song that caught my ear was "Inside."

10. Jules Massenet, "Meditation From 'Thais,'" composed in 1893 (5:05) from the Fabulous Philadelphia Sound Series, 1970. Philadelphia Orchestra, Eugene Ormandy.
One of the most gorgeous pieces of music ever composed. I recall finding this LP at Lovell's in September of 1970, right at the beginning of my college career. And so, I did all my early college assignments while playing this album of extremely beautiful music. The Meditation is from an opera and is liable to give one goose bumps while listening.

11. Gentle Giant, "Design," from Interview, 1976. (5:00)
This is not the first time I have chosen the interesting music of Gentle Giant. Dennis F bought this LP in the Bicentennial summer of 1976

at Lovell's and then played it for me in his little house in the back on Broadway Street. I recall sitting at his kitchen table, drinking tea and listening to this amazing array of highly technical progressive rock pieces, played by guys who had obviously mastered their respected instruments. I recall the most interesting piece was "Design."

PLAYLIST #21
"IGOR STRAVINSKY AND THE RITE OF SPRING"

SHORT BIO

IGOR STRAVINSKY (1882-1971). His father sang bass with an opera company, and thus provided young Igor with a solid musical background and influence. At first Igor was thinking of a career in law, but tried his hand at composition. He studied under the great genius Rimsky-Korsakov, and then finally was discovered by Diaghilev. He became an over-night celebrity with the debut of his Firebird ballet in 1910. He further cemented his hold as the greatest of all 20th Century composers with perhaps the 2 greatest works of the last one hundred years: Petrushka in 1911, and the Rite of Spring in 1913. He lost all his possessions during the Russian Revolution in 1918 and lived for a time in France. He eventually moved to the USA in 1939 and spent the rest of his life composing shorter, less ambitious pieces of music.

I well recall the day Stravinsky died in 1971. I was coincidentally working on a research paper about Stravinsky for my college music history class when I heard the news on my radio.

THE PLAYLIST:

1. Walt Disney Fantasia "Rite of Spring (1940) (approx. 21:00)
2. Igor Stravinsky The Rite of Spring (Le Sacre Du Printemps) (composed 1910 – 1911) Version for two pianos; interpreted by Michael Boyd and

MIND TAVERN

Joel Schoenhals (33.00)
Part I: The Adoration of the Earth (Day)
Part II: The Sacrifice (Night)

COMMENTARY:

Savage, brash, violent, barbaric, insane, outrageous, ingenious, unforgettable; a musical experience that transcends all other musical experiences for the serious audiophile. This pretty much sums up my feelings about Stravinsky's masterwork – *The Rite of Spring*.

I first heard this magnum opus in 1970 as part of my Music Appreciation course at Rio Hondo College, and back then as an 18 year old, I was basically shell-shocked and highly turned off by the intense ferocity of its various dissonant orchestral sounds and its complex array of dizzying poly-rhythms. Frankly, I had never heard anything like it before, and although I enjoyed the sublime oboe solo at the beginning, I never hung around to listen to the rest of the piece in its entirety. The music developed into something that literally hurt my ears if I turned up the volume too much.

As the years ensued, I knew of this piece. but I was never pulled toward its vast musical riches; was never compelled to find the inherent wealth this piece affords. After all, there was Chopin, Beethoven, Satie, Debussy, Mahler, Bach, Ravel and all the other masters to explore. But Stravinsky; I knew that this guy's music would require serious study on my part in order to finally appreciate it. I must admit it took Walt Disney to push me into the universe of Igor, When I saw Disney's animated interpretation in the Fantasia film from 1940, I began to change my feelings about this piece, thanks to all those primeval images of volcanoes erupting, and dinosaurs stomping and roaming the earth at will.

It was not until I listened to Stravinsky's Petrouchka in 1990 that I developed a strong affinity with the music of this amazing composer.

Naturally, after studying Petrouchka for 20 years, (I now listen to at least part of it everyday of my life without fail) I decided to give the "Rite" a serious scrutiny. I have not been disappointed. It is simply an amazing work of art.

Currently I possess four different recorded versions of Le Sacre; the absolute best being the Detroit Symphony Orchestra version, under the capable baton of Antal Dorati. His interpretation is absolutely amazing in its relentless tempos and mind-bending volume. It is truly outrageous in every way. After first hearing this tour de force performance, I could well understand why that first Parisian audience in 1913 literally rioted upon hearing it. There had never been anything like it before. When I listen to Le Sacre, which is often these days, I turn the volume high and simply bask in its universe of dense diverse chords and the myriad mental images these sounds evoke. And I invariably ask myself: How is it possible that a mere human being, albeit a genius, could invent such a collection of extraordinary sounds? Indeed, Igor was tapped into the Muse for this one.

For this playlist, I have included a different version of this work, a perspective that most aficionados of this piece do not often hear. This version is performed on two pianos by Michael Boyd and Joel Schoenhals. Initially, Stravinsky wrote the entire score for piano, and then later orchestrated it for the ballet performance. Structurally, the ballet is divided into two parts, all with the ancients dancing ritualistically in celebration of the new spring and the regeneration of life. The Rite though, involves the ritualistic killing of a virgin girl as a sacrifice, and it is at this point the music is at its most intense. Then after a build-up of erupting sounds and dissonant thuds, the music comes to a shuddering climax.

PLAYLIST #22
"THE GREATEST ROCK AND ROLL BAND OF ALL TIME"

THE ROLLING STONES — Mick Jagger, Keith Richards, Bill Wyman, Charlie Watts and Brian Jones— an amazing array of talent and gumption.

I first heard the music of The Rolling Stones sometime in late 1963 or early 1964, on KRLA radio. I dug their style and I liked Mick Jagger as a vocalist. I can also recall seeing them on TV's Shindig in 1965, and the Ed Sullivan Show a couple times during the mid to late 60's, playing their latest hits. And even though they were good, I was not all that excited about them. To be honest, I liked other bands better.

For many years as a music fan and collector, I have explored the universe of sounds; from Rock to Classical, from Jazz to the Blues, from Avant-garde to Ethnic; from the very old to the very new. And during all those years I never really explored, in-depth, the fascinating and, above all, fun music of this "Top Brick" group from England.

Yes, I had three of their albums back then: *12 X 5*, *Let It Bleed* and *Get Yer Ya Yas Out*, and I dug them as a 19 year old, quasi-hippie. But I think what really turned me off to the Stones was the album design for Sticky Fingers. I thought at the time it was for gays, and I quickly turned my interests to other musical groups and genres instead. But what a big mistake.

Because of Jeff K's encouragement in further exploring the music of the Stones, coupled with the fact that I knew another close friend was in the midst of his own personal exploration and rediscovery of this amazing group, I decided to do the same thing. So off to amazon.Com I go and

I purchased Jeff K's recommendations: Beggars Banquet, Sticky Fingers, and Exile On Main Street. I also purchased Aftermath and Between The Buttons. These were albums I refused to buy for almost 40 years. And when I listened to some of these songs for the first time, I was amazed at what I had been missing all these years. I could kick myself.

For this playlist I include my personal favorites from the aforementioned albums— 35 minutes of Rolling Stones music that I have newly discovered for the first time. For this list, I have not included any songs from albums I have had since the 60's; songs I have heard on the radio down through the years, or any songs from the Hot Rocks Anthology album, released in the late '80's. These pieces are absolutely new musical finds for me. Are The Rolling Stones the greatest Rock and Roll band of all time? After finding these treasures, I'd say, "probably yes." But I do not pretend to be a Rolling Stones expert, so my comments are few, and void of any amazing insights. I will leave those words of wisdom to the millions of musical scientists present in the world today.

1. "Doncha Bother Me," (2:48) from *Aftermath* (1966)
I love the rag-tag blues sound in this piece. Nice vocal by Mick.

2. "Flight 505" (3:27) from *Aftermath* (1966)
The piano introduction is cool and the ensuing jam is even better. Supposedly, this song is based on the flight number of Buddy Holly's death plane. Ian Stewart plays piano on this very cool piece. The Fuzzbass by Wyman definitely stands out.

3. "Its Not Easy" (2:56) from *Aftermath* (1966)
I think this is a great rocker— the Stones at their grittiest.

4. 'Cool, Calm & Collected" (4:12) from *Between The Buttons* (1967)
A somewhat eccentric piece with some great guitar and vocal work.

5. "Miss Amanda Jones" (2:47) from *Between The Buttons* (1967)
This is another incomparable recording. Keith's guitar is superb, and Mick is in complete command of his vocal phrasings. The Beatles could rock out with the best of them, especially with John on rhythm guitar. But the Beatles do not come close to this rock gem by Mick and Company.

6. "Parachute Woman" (2:20) from *Beggars Banquet* (1968)
There is great guitar playing on this song, with Dave Mason on lead guitar. Just before the guitar solo, Mick yells "Dave!" Amazing slide guitar by either Keith or Brian. A truly great find after all these years.

7. "Prodigal Son" (2:51) from B*eggars Banquet* (1968)
This is a great Delta Blues piece, written by Robert Wilkins, a Delta-blues guitarist from the 20's and 30's. Keith's virtuoso Delta Blues style is the highlight of this one.

8. "Dead Flowers" (4:13) from *Sticky Fingers* (1971)
I'm pretty sure Mick was thinking of Brian when he penned this. Apparently Mick did not take C&W music seriously, so this has some humorous overtones attached. A great song.

9. "Sister Morphine" (5:31) from *Sticky Fingers* (1971)
There's a nice build-up in this piece, and the guitar work has a cool gritty sound to it. Keith at his best. Mick's girlfriend, Marianne Faithful, wrote the lyrics, and, hence is responsible for the drug references.

10. "Pass The Wine" (Sophia Loren) (4:54) from *Exile On Main Street* (1972)
This is definitely one of my all-time favorites of the Stones. A great rock out. According to my research on this piece, it was not part of the LP back in 1972, but was added by the Guys in 2010 as an updated inclusion.

11. "Turd On The Run" (2:36) **from *Exile On Main Street* (1972)**
A great song to end this playlist. Jagger was quoted as saying about *Exile*: "This album is fucking mad." Just listen to this rock-out and I'm sure you'll concur with him.

PLAYLIST #23
"THE MOODY BLUES"
The Best of 1967 – 1972

THE MOODY BLUES:
Graeme Edge – drums, percussion
John Lodge – bass, guitar, vocals
Justin Hayward – guitar, vocals
Ray Thomas – vocals, flute, percussion, harmonica
Mike Pindar – keyboards, vocals

WHAT A DAUNTING TASK it was to come up with 35 minutes of what I consider to be the best of The Moody Blues. I wanted to keep my search centered on the early years, (1967 to 1972), and specifically the first 7 albums. I can recall first hearing this tight British rock group in 1967 on the radio, and I immediately liked their unusual but very catchy sound. It had a classical music bent to it at times, and it reminded me of some of the Beatles great songs from Revolver and Sgt. Pepper. "Nights in White Satin" and "Tuesday Afternoon" were two of those early pieces to which I developed an affinity, and probably heard a thousand times down through the years, and I still enjoy hearing them once in a blue moon. But for this playlist, I tried to steer away from the popular songs I heard on the radio all the time, and offer up what I consider to be the most interesting and musically satisfying pieces of their first half decade. Of course, it is merely my opinion that the following 8 songs represent the absolute quintessence of the great Moody Blues Sound. I am sure there are detractors, and they may speak their disagreements.

MIND TAVERN

1. "Leave This Man Alone," from Days of Future Passed (2:58) 1967
"Why am I so lonely?
Tell me is it right? (Is it right?)
Leave them, leave them, leave them, leave those things alone."
I listen to this piece and I think back to those old days of 1967 as a frightened, insecure freshman at Whittier High School, and actually believing girls had penises. Thank God my mother set me straight on that one. And I remember sitting in English class that year and checking out the blonde babe, Sandy S, sitting with legs crossed in the other row, and wishing she would be my "surfer girl." But alas, the prayers of that 15 year old boy went unheard in 1967 when the Moody Blues were becoming popular. And the blonde babe, Sandy S, whom I am sure is a grandmother by now, indeed, did leave this man alone. I love the guitar sound on this very cool, early rocker.

2. "Legend of a Mind," from In Search of the Lost Chord (6:36) 1968
"Along the coast you'll hear them boast
About a light they say that shines so clear.
So raise your glass, we'll drink a toast
To the little man who sells you thrills along the pier."
I first heard about drugs from my mother in 1963. I was 11 years old and living on Mavis Street. One day in the kitchen of our modest tract home, my aproned mother said to me: "You stay away from Jim Town. Mexicans there are dangerous, They smoke that marijuana stuff. It can make you high." "What's that?" "You lose your mind and you can die." In 1968 when this great song was written, the whole country was experiencing the Big Shift, from reactionary to radical. Millions, mainly our generation, were "tuning in and turning on," as Timothy Leary put it— and my very conservative mother was appalled by this emerging depravity in the world. This is perhaps the Moody's #1 drug song from the psychedelic 60's. A great tune that takes me back. And yes, Timothy Leary is dead.

3. "Voices in the Sky" from In Search of the Lost Chord (3:28) 1968
"Just what is happening to me
I lie awake with the sound of the sea
Calling to me."
Some really nice poetry in this song, and Ray Thomas' flute made this piece commercially popular. (I said I <u>tried</u> to steer away from the popular pieces). When I hear this, I think of my first girlfriend Teresa back in 1968... the two of us driving in my dad's chevy Impala, her sitting close to me on that wide front seat, cruising complacently through Whittier in the darkness, looking for neon lights. I can recall hearing this piece on the radio. Life then was so simple and easy and magical. Like this song is—
"If you could talk to me, what news would you bring?"

4. "Never Comes the Day" from On the Threshold of a Dream (4:43) 1969
"If only you knew what's inside of me now,
You wouldn't want to know me somehow.
But you will love me tonight.
We alone will be alright,
In the end."
This is definitely one of my top 3, all-time best Moody Blues songs. When I hear this piece, I think back to 1969, being 17 years old and living in the greatest, freest country the world had ever known. We went to the moon that summer and The Beatles would release Abbey Road shortly thereafter. Nixon was running the show and John Wayne was still alive and ready to kick America's enemies in the ass, at least on screen as Rooster Cogburn. When Labor Day strode in, I decided to break up with my girlfriend, and I did it on the phone. I planned it all summer, and I remember it was the saddest, lowest thing I had ever done. This song pretty much sums up my feelings about that break-up, and how life just goes on despite confusions and heartbreak, and that everything will be all right in the end.

5. "I Never Thought I'd Live to Be a Hundred," "Beyond," from, To Our Children's Children's Children, (4:04) 1969

"I never thought I'd have my freedom.
An age ago my maker was refusing me
The pleasure of the view."

I first heard these two pieces on KNAC FM radio, sometime in 1970. I was a senior at Whittier High School, and the blonde babe, Sandy S, had transferred to Sierra High. Along about the time I first heard these great songs, I had this strange dream that I have always remembered, I recall that I had walked outside my Hoover Street house at night and I saw a bright light come shooting out of the sky. This bright light enveloped me completely and inside this light, I saw her standing there, the blonde babe, Sandy S. herself, under that bright beam of light, and I went to be with her in that dream. These great songs from Children's Children will always remind me of that dream I had as a 18 year old, way back to another time and another world.

6. "It's Up to You," from A Question of Balance (3:11) 1970

"In the sadness of your smile love is an island way out to sea,
But it seems so long ago we have been ready trying to be free."

I like the country/rock feel to this piece. Fabulous guitar work and superb vocals. As I listen to this piece from the fall of 1970, I can well remember driving to Lovell's in my VW bug, sometimes with Marilyn riding shotgun. I remember getting this album at Lovell's that fall, and I remember it being a cold winter. So there we were, more often than not, cozy by the fireplace in the Hoover Street house, playing Moody Blues' A Question of Balance.

7. "Procession," from Every Good Boy Deserves Favour (4:40) 1971

"Desolation
Creation
Communication"

This piece is quite abstract with an eclectic assortment of interesting sounds. It reminds me of the Beach Boys' Good Vibrations, or perhaps The Beatles' "Number Nine."
(The funeral procession back in 1971 included many cars, as the lead hearse transported Mrs. B's body to the cemetery. I was driving my VW bug on the 60 Freeway, and Marilyn was riding shotgun. The procession lasted a half hour, and they buried her body deep into the ground, there in Resurrection Cemetery in San Gabriel).

8. "You and Me," from Seventh Sojourn (4:20) 1972
"You're an ocean full of faces
And you know that we believe
We're just a wave that drifts around you
Singing all our hopes and dreams."
Definitely one of the Moody's better rockers. The combination of Justin Hayward's guitar and Mike Pindar's mellotron gives this piece its distinctive sound. When I hear this piece, I remember back to a different time and a different country. I remember in 1972 I had a beard and a college degree. And I had a cool VW bug. I felt that the world was mine and I wasn't afraid of anything. My bravura about life at that time is aptly characterized by the melodic and rhythmic bravura of this great song. (All lyrics, copyright 1967-1972 by The Moody Blues)

PLAYLIST #24
"SALUTE TO THE JIMI HENDRIX EXPERIENCE"

THE EXPERIENCE:
James Marshall "Jimi" Hendrix (born Johnny Allen Hendrix) Lead Guitar, vocals, lyrics and music, (except #7).
November 27, 1942 – September 18, 1970
"American musician, singer, and songwriter, he is widely regarded as one of the most influential electric guitarists in the history of popular music, and one of the most celebrated musicians of the 20th century." (Wikipedia)
Noel Redding – Bass Guitar, vocals,
December 25, 1945 – May 11, 2003
"He would typically lay down a bass groove which Hendrix and drummer Mitch Mitchell would loosely play on top of. " (Wikipedia)
Mitch Mitchell – Drums
July 9, 1947 – November 12, 2008
"Mitchell's ability to provide an inspiring rhythmic platform for the pre-eminent guitar groundbreaker of his day, stands alongside Ringo Starr's accomplishment of providing a vital, creative, but ultimately supportive role with the Beatles." (Wikipedia)

COMMENTARY:

DURING ALL THE YEARS of creating playlists, I always had it in the back of my mind to do a list centering on the music of Jimi Hendrix and The Experience. And why not? As a teenager I dug Hendrix and his electric experience of weird guitar sounds that pulsated and gyrated in ways I had not heard before. And I liked his rock and roll style with bass and drums, all of it mixing in with psychedelic flourishes here and there. He was different and exciting, and legendary with the way he played. He was a "lefty," fast, edgy, but smoothly polished technically; sometimes he played with his teeth, and sometimes with the distorted sounds of the wah-wah pedal. He invariably added theatrics to his performances by setting his guitar on fire with lighter fluid. And I liked that part of Hendrix, the showman with style, taking it to the limit. Idiosyncrasies aside, Hendrix changed the face of rock music in the late 60's and he definitely deserves a spotlight. So this list contains what I think is his best stuff from the Experience's second and third albums: Axis: Bold As Love, and Electric Ladyland.

FROM: AXIS: BOLD AS LOVE (1967):

1. "Exp" (1:54)
"Good evening, ladies and gentlemen, Welcome to Radio Station EXP…"

This is Hendrix"s interesting introduction to the Axis album. Mitch Mitchell provides the voice for the announcer and Jimi plays Mr. Carusoe. We are led to believe Jimi has contacted an alien. Research seems to indicate that Hendrix was an avid believer in UFO's, and so, this is his telling reminder that, "you just can't believe everything you see and hear."

2. "Up From the Skies" (3:01)
This is a catchy song from side one that demonstrates Hendrix's cool jazzy style on guitar. Quite a contrast from his hard, ass-kicking rock style that he is known for. And his lyrics tell an interesting story of an extraterrestrial returning to Earth and being concerned with the damage caused by humans since the last time this alien passed through.

"I have lived here before, the days of ice. And of course this is why I'm so concerned."

3. " If 6 Was 9" (5:36)

Made ever famous by its inclusion in the counter culture classic film: Easy Rider. But I dug this piece and played it constantly on my record player in 1969, long before I ever saw the film. Great "acid-fueled blues" guitar licks on this piece along with special effects utilizing slap echo, fuzzbox distortion and reverb. Interestingly, Hendrix also played recorder on this piece. No doubt a "stoner's" delight.

"Now if 6 turned out to be 9, I don't mind, I don't mind. Alright, if all the hippies cut off all their hair, I don't care, I don't care."

4. "You Got Me Floatin'" (2:44)

Hendrix and The Experience at their jamming best. I recall being surprised that this Hendrix song never made it big commercially from copious amounts of radio play. At least I don't recall hearing this one on the radio. Allmusic describes the song as the "purest pop song" in Hendrix's body of work.

"Now your Daddy's cool, and your mamma's no fool, They both know I'm head over heels for you."

5. "Little Miss Lover" (2:20)

This is one of the more interesting pieces from Axis because it showcases Hendrix's sensual guitar style; In this obviously sexual song, we are led to understand that Jimi is about to score some snatch, and he is going to use his guitar to do so. This particular song was "the first to feature a percussive muted wah-wah effect (with the fretboard) – a technique that was later adopted by many guitarists." (Wikipedia)

"Excuse me while I see if the gypsy in me is right, If you don't mind."

FROM ELECTRIC LADYLAND (1968):

6. "And The Gods Made Love" (1:21)

Special effects in the studio by Jimi and the guys. I suppose this is a fitting introduction to perhaps the best album in the history of rock music, by one of the "gods" of rock.

"And he blurted out the sound, burst the side of his inner wall, also passing by, and the liquid rainbow melted Eros all through his rooms."

7. "Come On (Part 1)" (Earl King) (4:09)

I would like to play this rock and roll masterpiece immediately after the "Gods Made Love" track. For some deep sub-conscious reason, I think the two go together. Again, this is an excellent showcase of Hendrix at his technical best on the guitar. Of course this is Hendrix's cover of the 1960 recording by Earl King on Imperial Records.

"People talkin' but they just don't know, What's in my heart, and why I love you so, I love you baby like a miner loves gold, Come on sugar, let the good times roll, hey!"

8. "Voodoo Child (Slight Return) (5:12)

One of the monumental rock pieces of all time. If Joyce's *Ulysses* is the "Mt. Everest" of novels, then I humbly consider Hendrix's "Voodoo Child" to be the "Everest" of rock guitar recordings. It is five minutes of amazing virtuosity and talent.

"Well, I stand up next to a mountain, and I chop it down with the edge of my hand. And if I don't meet you no more in this world, then I'll meet you in the next one, And don't be late, don't be late…"

9. "1983 (A Merman I Should Turn To Be)" (13:39)

Hendrix had help from Chris Wood on flute for this psychedelic/apocalyptic journey to the bottom of the sea. Requiring 5 takes in the studio, Hendrix, along with producer, Eddie Kramer, produced some great effects with interesting tape loops and overdubs throughout, making this 1968 rock masterpiece one of almost "epic" proportions. It is the second longest recorded piece by The Experience.

"So my darling and I, make love in the sand, to salute the last moment, ever on dry land, our machine has done its work, played its part well, without a scratch on our bodies, and we bid it farewell."

(All lyrics, Copyright 1968, Experience Hendrix)

PLAYLIST #25
"THE 1960'S – DECADE OF TRANSCENDENCE"

1. **"New Orleans," Gary "U.S." Bonds (2:44) 1960**
I loved this piece when I was 8 years old. I was in second grade at St. Mary's School, getting ready for my First Holy Communion. I can recall hearing this on KFWB radio every morning and afternoon for that entire spring while riding in my parents' blue Chevy Impala to and from school with Patti M sitting close to me on the front seat. This piece has a raw edge to it with a tight beat; employing a "garage-rock"-type of sound. It also has a nice sax rift in it, and whenever I hear this piece i think of 8 year old Patti M and her creamy white legs.

2. **"I'm Sorry," Brenda Lee (2:40) 1960**
What a great simple tune this is. I have always thought that Brenda Lee was a major pop force when the transcendent '60's dawned. Possessed with a powerfully controlled voice, I put Brenda Lee right up there with Connie Francis, Judy Garland and Barbra Streisand even. Enjoy this pure "cheese" from 1960… "May it serve you well."

3. **"Blue Moon," The Marcels (2:17) 1961**
My family and I had just moved up to Redding California when this song shot to #1 on the radio. A very ear-catching, doo-wop piece with this weird "ba-bomp-bompa-bomp, danga-dang-dang, dinga-dong-ding blue moon" refrain in it. I suppose this was their shtick in order to get attention and air-time, and it was very successful with me at least.

4. "Walk Right Back," The Everly Brothers (2:18) 1961

When this piece was on the American Bandstand every day at 4:30, I was living in this big ranch house with the Sacramento River in the backyard. And everyday I was "riding double" on this roan named "Stormy" with 13 year old Darla H through Kirch's Field. Of all the Everly pieces, this one is my personal favorite. It has an insouciant, engaging sound to it, epitomizing the innocuously carefree early '60's… before the bullets of Dallas.

5. "Let's Dance," Chris Montez (2:15) 1962

This was a big favorite of mine back in '62. I learned to do "The Twist" to this song. Again I gravitated to rock pieces that were raw, unspoiled and sounded like they were recorded in someone's garage or basement. I remember thinking the organ sounded "cool" on this one, and it still is after all these years. It's weird how certain tunes bring photographic memories to mind. Well, for this one, it brings back times with my dad and brother fishing off Newport pier for sand sharks on a cool summer's evening.

6. "Hey! Baby," Bruce Channel (2:23) 1962

The harmonica is what makes this song! And I developed a strong liking for this little instrument because of Hey! Baby. I can recall being bed-ridden for 2 months with Bright's disease when this piece was #1 on the radio. Most of the time I would watch TV (Soupy Sales and Felix the Cat) and listen to the radio to wile away the time. I recall hating the Duke of Earl with a passion, but I loved this piece for its uncanny ability to always put me in a good mood.

7. "409," The Beach Boys (1:58) 1962

With the exception of Wipe Out by The Safaris, I wasn't too much into surf music in the early 60's. But I did dig this "hot rod" single by the "California Fab Five." I guess why I liked this rocker so much was because my brother was in a car club called the Aztecs, and all those guys were always in someone's garage, fixing up some late 40's "junker." And while those "older" high school guys were getting their hands greasy, KRLA was always playing in the background. I think 409 is simply one of the top five pieces by the Beach Boys. A very "California-sounding" piece of early 60's Americana. It brings back memories of going to the"Drags" with my brother down in Wilmington.

8. "He's So Fine," The Chiffons (1:50) 1963
When this song was constantly playing on KRLA during the late spring of 1963, I was the president of the Mavis Street Spy Club. And along with Kenny and Larry S, and big Dennis N, we would all go spying on our neighbors, peeking through old wooden fences in obscure suburban backyards, hoping to see anyone who happened to be naked. Life was wonderful back then and I truly felt that He's So Fine was the finest song I had ever heard up to that point in time.

9. "Do You Want To know A Secret," The Beatles (1:56) 1963
I was in the basement of my Hoover Street pad, listening to the Emperor Hudson show on KRLA, when I first heard The Beatles. And this was the first song by The Fab Four that entered into the external auditory canals of my ears. And when it did, my life changed forever. Sung by George, I immediately fell in love with its quaint rhythm and unique melody. I remember wanting to hear more by this British group with the weird name.

10. "Since I Fell For You," Lenny Welch (2:53) 1964
Since my brother and I always had KFWB radio playing back in the late 50's, I can recall developing a strong appreciation for pop vocalists like Elvis Presley, Paul Anka, Pat Boone, Andy Williams and Johnny Mathis. In 1964 this piece was played on KRLA and I immediately liked its emotional, angst-laden voicing by Lenny Welch. At the time, I was wooing this 12 year old girl named Carol Sue J who lived up the street from me and I could relate to its "cheesy"heartrending lyrics.

11. "Louie, Louie," The Kingsmen (2:45) 1964

First time I heard this song was in the summer of '64. I was playing on my skateboard in the backyard at Hoover Street, and my brother was in the garage working on an old, gray '46 Ford "junker" with four of his fellow Aztecs. Wearing blue jeans and white tee-shirts, the Aztecs smoked Marlboros when they weren't getting their hands greasy. And while they worked and smoked, they played KRLA loudly. The only time I can remember the Aztecs not working or smoking was when 'Louis, Louie' came on and that's when they began dancing with themselves. Later on, my brother informed me that the lyrics were obscene and he even wrote out a transcription of those risqué words that I could not understand when listening to the vocalist. I don't recall many of those words but I do recall the part of the song when he says: "I felt down low into her hair…" My mother never knew about those lyrics. Had she known, there would have been another California earthquake.

12. "Oxford Town," Bob Dylan (1:50) 1962

I first heard Bob Dylan when I was in the 7th grade. My brother was a senior at Whittier High and he recommended that I "try this guy." Oxford Town from his first LP was the first Dylan piece that I took to in an obsessive way. I loved the fluid guitar and the interesting, rhyming words dealing with racial bigotry. I suppose this song was sort of an epiphany to me— I came to the realization that music could be serious with a strong intellectual message, and not just some stupid, cheesy song about surfing or cruising or dancing.

13. "I'm Happy Just To Dance With You," The Beatles (2:00) 1964

I danced only twice with Carol Sue that October night, when Georgie M and I attended the Junior High Dance at Palm Park in 1964. The place was jammed with hormonal, newly pubescent teenagers who attended Dexter Junior High. The first song was Sugar Shack by Jimmy Gilmer and the Fireballs. This one, 'Happy To Dance' was the second song. I recall thinking how the words, sung by Beatle George, were…" oh so true…" about us… me and Carol Sue. I am convinced, after rehearing and studying all 13 EMI albums by the Fab Four, that this piece is from The Beatles' highest point, the apex, of their collective musical creativity. After Hard Day's Night, it was all downhill in my opinion.

14. "I Got You Babe," Sonny and Cher (3:11) 1965
In order to fully find out why I have included this "cheesy, rock schlock" by Sonny and Cher on this playlist, you must read chapter 8 of In-A-Gadda-Da-Vida, entitled "You Could Hypnotize Someone." When you do, then you'll understand. I loved this piece when it climbed to #1 in the summer of '65. I especially loved the oboe in it. I had never heard anything like it before.

15. "All Day And All of the Night," The Kinks (2:21) 1965
Mid-1960's hard rock at its best. At the time I thought the guitar playing was the best I had ever heard, and that included The Beatles, and even Dick Dale, the "King of the Surf Guitar" himself. I just wished that the guitar solo could have been longer. Whenever I heard this piece come on the radio while riding in my dad's beige Impala, I always asked him to "turn it up!"

16. "Subterranean Homesick Blues," Bob Dylan (2:19) 1965
My favorite Dylan piece definitely. I guess because KRLA played it all the time. I love the wild obscure poetry:
"Get sick get well,
Hang around an ink well,
Ring bell,
Hard to tell If anything is goin' to sell,
Try hard, get barred,
Get back, write braille,
Get jailed, jump bail, join the army, if you fail…"

I still don't know what Dylan's stream of consciousness-bending lyrics are talking about, but I do know his music was transcendent for the time.

17. "Going To A Go-Go," The Miracles (2:44) 1966

This is probably my all-time favorite "Motown" piece. This has great vocals by this dynamic men's group headed by "Smokey" Robinson. It has a driving almost hypnotic feel to it, and it conjures up tons of memories, both good and bad, of starting high school as a skinny punk freshman at Whittier High.

18. "Good Vibrations," Beach Boys (3:35) 1966

I remember being suitably impressed with this highly experimental piece by the California Fab Five. Seamlessly recorded, I still marvel at its rich musical textures and remarkable harmonies. Definitely Brian Wilson's" tour de force." When this piece was #1 on the radio, I thought it was the best song I'd ever heard.

19. "Paperback Writer," The Beatles (2:19) 1966

Basically it's impossible to pin down my #1 favorite Beatles piece. There are so many musical treasures in their repertory. It would be like choosing one pearl from out of a bowl containing hundreds. But if I had a gun pointed at me, and I was threatened with death if I didn't or couldn't decide on #1, I would probably pick Paperback Writer.

20. "The End," The Doors (11:33) 1967

I rank this outrageous piece by Jim Morrison and The Doors as #1 on my All-Time Rock List. The poetry is superb with vivid, unforgettable imagery and, of course, it startles you with its obvious Oedipal overtones. I can recall playing this piece over and over again on my little blue record player inside my Hoover Street bedroom back in 1967, and my conservative mother angrily asking me about the part when Jim says: "Father, I want to kill you." She thought it was "trash." I begged to differ.

21. "If 6 Was 9," Jimi Hendrix Experience (5:32) 1968

"I'm gonna wave my freak flag high!" I guess this piece, along with Voodoo Child (slight return), are my all-time favorites of Jimi Hendrix. I was completely blown away by his music. And no one has played the rock guitar better, before him or since. This one is from his second LP, "Axis: Bold As Love" which includes some great "headphone" pieces. Transcendent, psychedelic rock at its late 60's finest.

22. "Dazed And Confused," Led Zeppelin (6:26) 1968

Another highly transcendent hard rock song from a group introduced to me by Dave B. I was wowed by the guitar virtuosity of Jimmy Page. This piece basically kicks ass as it sears and tears at your listening consciousness. A great one for headphones. I was a senior at Whittier High, and I recall coming home from school everyday and blasting this piece at full volume on my stereo. It was a rush.

23. "In-A-Gadda-Da-Vida," Iron Butterfly (17:05) 1968

I finish my playlist with this very transcendent song… the song that my entire novel centers on … 17 minutes of continuous music…absolutely unheard of before 1968, with the exception of The End by the transcendent Doors. The drum solo is hypnotic and compelling; I can still see my girlfriend, Terri, dancing in front of me as Ron Bushy, the drummer, conjures visions of Edenic love-making with his tight drumming style. The organ solo by Doug Ingle is absolutely mesmerizing, reminding me of someone playing softly in a church before the beginning of Mass. Very spiritual indeed, but one could also perhaps see the serpent as it slinks in the shadows of ancient Eden. At any rate, an extremely memorable piece for me. Read my novel and it will all come to light.

PLAYLIST #26
"A YOU TUBE EXPERIENCE"

LAST SUMMER WHEN DENNIS F came to visit me in The Cave, we both stumbled, so to speak, upon a new and very interesting format or theme for our Listening Sessions – Using YouTube videos. For the better part of that day, we took turns downloading video after fascinating video of great music and performances. And what made it so great was the fact that Dennis F hooked up our computers with his stereo system, providing an amazingly dynamic soundscape with which to watch the performances. It was then that I came straight out and asked if we could somehow do this particular format again up in Danford Canyon in October. The Dude then gave me the green light to at least try it. So without further ado, and after over 15 hours of preparation, here is my YouTube playlist experience:

1. Johnny Crawford and Peter Mintun, "When the Folks High Up Do the Mean Low-Down," composed by Irving Berlin (3:17) video recorded in 1993.
I start this YouTube Experience with Mark McCain, er…Johnny Crawford in his late 40's, singing this very catchy piece from an Irvin Berlin musical of the 1930's. All I can say is Crawford has come a long way since singing "Greensleeves" to that cute blond babe on one of the last Rifleman episodes in 1963. I simply like this piece and wanted to share Crawford's mature and obvious singing talent.

2. Jean Luc Ponty, "Individual Choice," video recorded in 1983, (3:38)

I first saw this interesting video back in 1984 on cable TV while living on Broadway Street in Whittier. I was drawn in by the engaging hypnotic modernist intonations of Ponty's soundscapes and the speeded up perspectives of the various landscapes as depicted in the video. The video looks antique by today's HD standards, but it is still quite cool.

3. "Pipe Dream" by Animusic.Com (3:38)

This is a very clever video opus which includes percussion sounds with jazz elements. There is quite a sizable catalogue of interestingly ingenious videos on YouTube by Animusic. Highly recommended.

4. Vaughn Williams, Tuba Concerto, Movement Two – "Romanza," Aaron Tindall- Tuba.

I wanted to include this second movement from Vaughn Williams' Tuba Concerto on this playlist because it is simply a fabulously beautiful piece. The visual, unfortunately, is static, just a picture of the soloist. But this second movement is expertly rendered and a joy to hear.

5. Jeff Buckley, "Dream Brother," with Salvador Dali Art Montage (4:45)

This montage of Dali artwork goes perfectly with Buckley's "Dream Brother." Of all the music performed by the late Buckley, I would say this piece is his best. But this is just my opinion. I have had a 40 year fascination with the surreal art of Dali; it is so Freudian and yet realistic in a dream-like way. I recall spending hours back in the 70's looking at his pieces inside my old office on Hoover Street, mesmerized and awe-struck by his incredible talent.

6. "Avant-Garde Electronic Music Meditations," Brice Salek (2:55)

Get set for some strangeness with this piece. This is "wacked out" at its best. Great sounds from somewhere in the cosmos, and the visuals are simply indescribable. A nightmare right out of 1953.

7. "Sonya!" Best Belly Dancing On YouTube (5:31)

May I present Sonya, the belly dancer. Even though she puts on an amazing performance here, and is gorgeously beautiful, it is not Sonya who must be watched and appreciated in this video. It is the guy in black sitting on the chair playing the conga drum, who must be seen and heard to be believed. This is by far the best belly dance performance I have seen yet on YouTube. And the conga playing is flawless and incredibly eclectic in its array of various rhythms. Both are obviously the best in the business.

8. Braindrop, "Avant Garde Symphony" and "Frequency Shifter" (5:01)

It's too bad this video creation was not around in the 60's and early 70's. All the stoners would have grooved out on this one. Let it take you away into the world of psychedelia.

9. Poulenc, "Trois Novelettes," Jocelyn Freeman- piano, (7:30)

Recently I have been rediscovering the highly interesting piano music of Francis Poulenc, of the French Les Six. I found this excellent performance by a very ravishing Jocelyn Freeman on piano. I am sure you guys will agree that both piece and performer are not devoid of any pulchritudinous overtones.

10. Terry Riley, "A Rainbow in Curved Air," composed in 1969, (18:00)

This is the highlight piece of this playlist. The music is superb and highly engaging to hear. As you experience this Riley signature piece from 1969, you will be traveling through outer space and the cosmos, seeing all the sights as if you were flying freely in spirit. Eventually you will make your way to Planet Earth and will find yourself traveling above the ground at a great speed, like some UFO craft surveying the planet. Then you will land in the Holy Land, all of this in HD. I first heard "Rainbow" at Cal State Fullerton in 1973 and was astounded by it.

11. Satie, "La Diva de l'Empire," (3:00)
I found this gem in the Satie section and was immediately charmed by the ultra sexy Mary-Liz O'Neill, the mezzo-soprano for this piece. But of course it is not O'Neill's obvious sex appeal and outstanding singing that redeems this musical masterpiece, no, it is the great piano playing by the plump lady with the glasses, Rosemary Ritter, that sends our musical souls soaring.

12. Frank Sinatra, "One For My Baby (And One More for the Road) (4:37) 1958
I couldn't think of a better way to end this YouTube experience. Ol' Blue Eyes drowning his sorrows at Joe's Bar at 3 in the morning. *"Make it one more for my baby, and one more for the road."* And Frank himself will have one more thing to say to end this playlist:
"*Good night. Sleep warm.*"

PLAYLIST #27
"20 COMPELLING 'HEADPHONE' ALBUMS"

In 2016 I decided to listen to one music album every day for one work week, while driving to and from my teaching job in Whittier, a 25-mile journey. I called these weekly listening reviews: "Commuter Music," and all were initially published on Facebook. This final playlist includes 20 of the Commuter Music album reviews.

Pink Floyd - The Dark Side of the Moon (1973)
Amazing album. I played 'Dark Side' by Pink Floyd 8 times during this week, and the best word I can come up with to describe it is "delicious," especially the pieces "The Great Gig in the Sky" and "Any Color You Like." It is the ultimate "headphone" album, with outstanding arrangements and musicianship. You'll think you have taken off into the higher stratospheres, heading for the center of the universe while listening to this masterpiece. If I'm not mistaken, I read years ago this album was created and recorded exclusively for the use of "headphones." As a metaphor, I don't doubt that at all. Highly recommended for 'Heads' too. A+. "I will see you on the dark side of the moon."

The Clash - London Calling (1980)
I have been wanting to play this classic album for a very long time, and so, I happily played it 7 times this week. Expecting to hear a lot of typical punk rock pieces on this highly acclaimed album, instead I heard an eclectic offering of 19 songs which ranged from rockabilly to rock 'n'

roll; from reggae to R & B. And these boys can rock out indeed. The best song on this highly recommended album is "Brand New Cadillac" a truly scorching rocker composed by Mick Jones and Joe Strummer. Other standout pieces in my opinion include "Jimmy Jazz" (with a very cool walking bass), "Rudy Can't Fail" and "Lost in the Supermarket." Overall, I enjoyed hearing this album, ranked #8 by Rolling Stone in its Top 500.

Miles Davis - Bitches Brew (1970)
This is an amazing album indeed. I was absolutely enthralled with the sheer ferocity of this music. Miles Davis and a host of musical sidemen produce one of the most electrifying albums I have ever heard. It is essential to hear this amazing album on headphones. I played this two-disc set 7 times this week, and discovered the magic of jazz rock fusion, ala Miles Davis. My favorite on this album is "Spanish Key" which includes an amazing jam session with astonishing playing by Davis on trumpet and Bennie Maupin on bass clarinet. Chick Corea provides a dynamic bottom on electric piano. My other favorites include. "Bitches Brew," a 26-minute jazz rock explosion, and "Miles Runs the Voodoo Down," with Miles delivering his best trumpet playing on the album. I have been curious about this album for many years, and now I finally had a chance to enjoy this masterpiece. A+   Highly recommended

Derek and The Dominos - Layla and other assorted love songs (1970)
Had a great time listening to this early 70's classic with Eric Clapton and Duane Allman on guitars , Bobby Whitlock on keyboards, Jim Gordon on percussion and Carl Radle on bass. I was astonished at just how eclectic this album is. It has an array of blues, hard and soft rock songs that are catchy and cool to hear. My favorites are "Have You Ever Loved a Woman," a great blues piece with some electrifying blues guitar by Eric and Duane; "Why Does Love Got To Be Sad," another great blues piece, "Thorn Tree in the Garden," a beautiful quiet song, sung by Duane,

and finally, my favorite, "Tell the Truth." The guys on this piece put it all together and accomplished one of the best jams I have heard ever. I remember seeing this LP at Lovell's in Whittier, but never picked it up. 46 years later I finally gave this classic a good week-long listen. I played this 14-song album eight times this week and enjoyed their excellent musical offerings. It is perfect music for headphones. It seemed the band really enjoyed themselves making this album. I loved it, so I give Layla an A grade.

The Byrds - Younger Than Yesterday (1967)
Fabulous album indeed. One of the best albums for headphones. It was so good I think I played it way too many times and got sick of it. Still, this is simply great psychedelic rock, with every song being exhilaratingly enjoyable to hear. My favorites being: "My Back Pages," "So You Want To Be a Rock 'n' Roll Star," "Have You Seen Her Face" and my #1 favorite song: "Mind Gardens," composed and sung by David Crosby. It goes without saying that I loved this classic album. A+

The Zombies - Odessey and Oracle (1968)
This album turned out to be a major discovery for me. I had never heard of it, until recently, while reading about in Rolling Stone's Top 500 Albums book, and I whole-heartedly agree: After hearing it 14 times this week, this is indeed a great album. Rod Argent and Chris White penned 12 highly engaging and "summery fun" type pieces that definitely take one back to simpler times. Besides their hit, "Time of The Season," this compelling collection includes a smattering of even better songs, 2-to-3-minute musical gems I had never heard before: ""Care of Cell 44," "A Rose for Emily," "Beechwood Park" and my number 1 favorite, "Butchers Tale." This album is excellent in every sense of the word. A+

If you are a "Boomer," and have not heard this somewhat obscure album from 1968 yet (like me), it is highly recommended. "Whose your daddy?"

Blood, Sweat & Tears (1968)

Outstanding jazz/rock compilation. I never really appreciated these guys when I was loving rock music back in the late 60's. But after playing this great album 9 times, I discovered perhaps the best jazz rock keyboard performance of all time. Included on this CD is a Live version of Smiling Phases with the dazzling playing of Dick Halligan on electric piano. This piece alone is worth the price of the CD. It is highly recommended and play it loud to get the full effect of the rich horn section and a dynamic bass by Jim Fielder. A+.

Steely Dan - Aja (1977)

This classic best seller of late 70's jazz rock fusion, came highly recommended to me by a friend, so I gave it 8 full listens. Although I was amazed at the highly polished craftsmanship of every song arranged by Donald Fagen and Walter Becker, and although I was in awe of the superb quality of the engineered recording itself, and although every song was masterfully executed by perhaps the best studio musicians at that time, I was happy, to be honest, when Friday at last arrived and I could stop listening to this "perfect" album. The problem I have with this "masterpiece" is that I have heard this music before, many times down through the years- at wedding receptions, inside dentist's waiting rooms, inside department stores on the Muzak PA system, restaurants and other places as well where you might hear it in the background. But I can also state unequivocally that I have never heard Steely Dan in an elevator, not yet. To put it bluntly, I became bored with this album after listening to it a few times. To quote the writer, Richard Connell: "There is nothing more boring than perfection." Nevertheless, I did have two favorites from this compilation of 7 songs: "Aja" is my number 1 favorite with some very catchy music and outstanding playing, especially the guitar, and " I Got the News" has some great jazz piano in it. Overall, I give this album an "A" grade, obviously, but I think it is one of those albums you play once a year, when in the mood. Recommended indeed.

Traffic (1968)

I recall seeing this album countless times at Lovell's record store while going through all those great rock LP's of the late 60's and early 70's. And never did I buy it. So, this week I decided to discover the songs of Traffic, a very cool band of excellent musicians. Stevie Winwood plays a superb organ on all 10 songs, especially on "Crying To Be Heard," my favorite from this enjoyable album. Dave Mason provides outstanding, hard rock guitar prowess on "Pearly Queen." His guitar has its own voice in all the songs and makes the music of Traffic unique and unforgettable. Chris Wood plays some amazing flute in all the jams with Jim Capaldi playing drums. My other favorites are "Feelin' Alright," "Don't Be Sad" and "You Can All Join In." I honestly love this album. Great songs indeed. I played this album 11 times this week and I highly recommend it. A+

Elton John - Goodbye Yellow Brick Road (1973)

I enjoyed these 17 songs by Elton and his excellent backing band. "Bennie and the Jets" is my personal favorite with "Candle in the Wind," "Harmony" and "Funeral for a Friend" as the stand-out pieces on this excellent compilation, ranked #91 by Rolling Stone in their book of Top 500 albums. Great breezy pop rock music here, circa early 70's style. It is a flawlessly recorded, performed and produced album. A true classic indeed. Grade A.

Van Morrison - Astral Weeks (1968)

I just spent an astral week listening to Van Morrison's masterpiece album, Astral Weeks. What can I say? This is a great album that I never would have purchased in 1968. It was not a hard rock band playing hard rock blues boogie. This music instead is lyrical and beautiful and utterly sublime. Morrison's vocals are at times soulful and ever-longing, but always reassuring and musically unique. Every song is great on this album, but my favorite is "Ballerina" with "Madame George," and "Cyprus Avenue" coming 2nd and 3rd. A+ Highly recommended music for headphones.

Johnny Cash at Folsom Prison (Recorded Live 1968)
I had been interested in hearing this Johnny Cash classic for many years since its release in 1968. And so, this week was the time to give it a good listen. This album is simply excellent. I especially enjoyed the banter between Johnny and the prisoners. He truly captivates his audience by showing those guys respect, and Johnny genuinely enjoys entertaining them, and this relationship is the reason why "Folsom" is one of the most interesting and entertaining albums of the 60's. Moreover, Cash's great singing with The Tennessee Three backing him with that Cash Signature sound, makes this album truly transcendent. I enjoyed all 19 songs immensely, especially "Folsom Prison Blues," "The Long Black Veil" and "Jackson." These were my personal likes or standouts, with "Cocaine Blues" being my favorite. June Carter momentarily steals the show when she sings with Johnny on "Jackson," putting in an amazing performance. Overall, I played this great vintage album 8 times this week and I grade it a solid "A."

Procol Harum - Broken Barricades (1971)
Guitarist, Robin Trower exhibits fine hard rock prowess on this very interesting album. Especially on the song "Memorial Drive." Other stand-out songs include "Simple Sister," "Power Failure" and "Song for a Dreamer." A very tight group indeed, displaying some of the best hard rock of the era. I played this 8 times this week and I recommend this album to aficionados of early 70's FM rock radio. Kick back!

Bruce Springsteen - Born To Run (1975)
Never been a "Bruce" fan.... until now. And when I played this album on Monday, I did not like it at all. But I kept playing it until Friday and I have now changed my mind. This is almost the "perfect" album, if that is possible. This has great musicianship and writing indeed. My favorites being: Thunder Road, Tenth Avenue Freeze-Out, Born To Run, and Meeting Across The River (with some very cool trumpet music). After hearing this great album all week, I understand now why there are

so many Bruce fans, because his music makes you feel that living life is worth living. There is unbridled joy in his passionate singing: His overall message being that life is tough at times, but it is all worth it in the long run. I am very happy to have discovered this vintage classic from Bruce's early days. Highly recommended. "I want to guard your dreams and visions..."

Neil Young and Crazy Horse - Live Rust (1978)
"Live Rust" by Neil Young is an outstanding Live album. I read about this album in the Rolling Stone Top 500 Albums book, and I admit I was sold by all the praise. Well, as it turned out, I was thoroughly entertained by this "Live" recording of some of Neil's finest songs. With the help of his Crazy Horse back-up band, consisting of Frank Sampedro on guitar, Billy Talbot on Bass and Ralph Molina on drums, I heard these classic performances 11 times this week, with "Sugar Mountain," "When You Dance I Can Really Love," "Cinnamon Girl" and "Tonight's The NIght" as my favorites. I was not much of a Neil Young fan back in the early 70's, except of course for his contributions to CSNY, but now I have a new appreciation for his vintage 70's music. Highly recommended indeed. I grade this a solid "A."

Bob Dylan-Bringing It All Back Home (1965)
I played this masterpiece 7 times this week, from Tuesday to Friday. This is thoroughly enjoyable music with great lyrics to boot. All the pieces are classics, but my favorite song, the one that most affirms my belief that life is tough but great, is "Mr. Tambourine Man." This is a 50/50 album with half the music being folk with Bob alone and then the other half is folk rock with electric guitar, bass and drums. This album also includes some classic lines of 1960's poetry: "Johnny's in the basement, mixing up the medicine." "Money doesn't talk, it swears." "The pump don't work 'Cause the vandals took the handles." Recommended to my socialist friends.

MIND TAVERN

John Mayall and the Blues Breakers with Eric Clapton (1966)
Very cool album indeed. Thoroughly enjoyed hearing this vintage British Blues band that ultimately made Clapton, and his outstanding guitar playing, famous. Every track displayed outstanding blues technique, especially "Parchman Farm," with great guitar by Clapton and some very cool harmonica playing by Blues Breaker founder, John Mayall. There were 12 songs on this album with "Hideaway," Ray Charles' "What'd I Say " and "It Ain't Right" as my favorites. This was another cool week listening to this very interesting forerunner to Cream, which changed the Rock World just a couple years later. Highly recommended, and most assuredly, essential listening if you dig the Blues. Grade A.

John Lennon - Imagine (1971)
This is an excellently composed, performed and recorded album. "Exceptional" might be a better word to describe John's Magnum Opus. Every piece is finely produced and well- crafted with John supplying the core of the sound on vocal, guitar and sometimes piano. And he gets amazing musical help from George Harrison, Klaus Voorman, Jim Keltner, Nicky Hopkins, Allan White and King Curtis on some very cool sax. This excellently produced album (Phil Spector) includes 11 songs that I heard 9 times this week. I was especially impressed with "It's So Hard," (a great rocker), "Oh Yoko," "Imagine," " and my favorite song: "I Don't Wanna Be a Soldier Mama I Don't Wanna Die." I find it amazing that it took me 45 years to buy and listen to this very cool album by one of the best— the disputed leader of the Beatles. Put on the headphones for this one.

Hank Williams Greatest Hits (Mercury recordings from 1947-1952)
Great compilation of the best in early 50's country music. Hank Williams signature sound of guitar, violin, bass, drums and the steel guitar, played expertly by R.D. Norred, with "Honky Tonk Blues" and "Hey Good Lookin'" being the standouts. I recommend this great vintage country music to those who hate country music. Play Hank Williams for a week,

and like me, you will be feeling great pity for this poor guy, who evidently experienced many romantic heartbreaks. And there is a heavy dose of poignancy attached to this music because of Hank's death at 29 in 1953.

Marvin Gaye - What's Going On (1971)
This is one of those albums that as a youth I tended to ignore because it was Motown, and therefore it was not hard rock and roll. But I have read several positive reviews of this Motown Classic down through the years, so I played it 5 times while cruising down the central coast of California today. Now I understand. Now I get it. This is indeed a great album simply because it has great music in it. "What's Going On," "Save The Children" and "Right On" are exhilarating to hear; the other songs are likewise masterfully crafted by a master craftsman. And Marvin Gaye's message behind all the fabulous music is stunning unto itself. I give this masterpiece an A+.

ADDENDA
"MIND TAVERN"

The Elvin Bishop Concert at Rio Hondo College, Whittier
January 23, 1971

It was a relatively cold January evening in 1971 when I ventured up to Rio Hondo College with Marilyn R, Dennis F, Chris B and Mike E to see Elvin Bishop live in concert. Wearing denim overalls, and with his hair askew in about thirty different directions, I thought Bishop and his backing band were one hell of a tight group. Playing mostly rock-gospel-blues type pieces, I remember being quite impressed with Bishop's range and smoothness on the guitar. Every piece in his set was fast paced, spirited and quite danceable, and I was also quite impressed with the organist— a long haired, bearded dude who complimented Bishop perfectly. Moreover, Bishop had a couple of sexy chicks wailing away on backing vocals for each piece, ironically giving the music a strong gospel feel to it.

    The concert took place in the spacious college cafe with at least two hundred college students hovering near the stage. I remember the room being quite dark that night except for the psychedelic strob lights that made it seem like everyone was experiencing the same LSD trip. Most of the guys present had long hair and bushy beards, and the chicks were primo "bitchin ass" types, with straight hair and no make-up. At that time, make-up was part of the "establishment," and therefore, "uncool," so the chicks looked very earthy and natural. One of those earthy chicks was my girlfriend, Marilyn R. All through the concert, Marilyn clapped her hands and moved her hips to the rhythms of Bishop's very cool music. That was righteous. We must have danced for two hours straight. Finally, the concert ended, and I remember walking to the parking lot and passing by the see-through windows of the faculty lounge where the band had retreated. Reclining on a chair, smoking a cigarette and looking exhausted, Elvin Bishop was oblivious to my distant stares.

The Mike Bloomfield Concert at The Golden Bear, Huntington Beach July 25, 1971

He was a pure bluesman—fluid, smooth as silk, passionate, intense. Mike Bloomfield could play blues guitar with the best of them. I saw this great musician from the front of that small stage at the old Golden Bear in Huntington Beach one warm summer evening in 1971. He played an old rickety Gibson guitar so smoothly that the crowd gave him several ovations. I don't remember his sidemen at all for the simple reason they paled in comparison.

Most of the pieces he played were from his album collaborations with Al Kooper. When Bloomfield played, 'Who Knows," you could hear a pin drop in the audience where I was sitting, if that's possible. Yeah, the music was loud, but not the crowd. No one made a sound, as if they were hypnotized by his amazing blues virtuosity. As he wailed on each song, the long haired chicks sitting by me were giving him the adulation I'm sure he had become accustomed to down through the years as a Chicago bluesman. I have often wondered if Mike scored that night with any of those tanned babes from Huntington Beach.

Throughout that small nightclub I could smell the unmistakable aroma of spaghetti and garlic bread as Bloomfield sweated through one great blues piece after another. I often wonder what became of all those long haired dudes and chicks that were present that night in that stuffy dark room.

I do know that one of the all-time best blues guitarists, Mike Bloomfield, died in 1981, ten short years after this very memorable concert at the old Golden Bear in Huntington Beach.

The Johnny Winter Concert at the Santa Monica Civic Auditorium September 2, 1970

As the great summer of 1970 came to a close, there was one event I had planned on attending before embarking on my college career: the September 2nd Johnny Winter concert at the Santa Monica Civic Auditorium. I had waited all summer for this concert and I decided I would take my favorite date at the time, Terri R.

Terri evidently was very psyched up for this date, for she went out and spent a considerable amount of money on a new dress, a slinky red one that clung to her body like sticky seran wrap. We traveled in my old red VW bug, the "Red Ball Jet," via the Santa Monica freeway through the worst part of Los Angeles to get to the concert. Terri sat next to me in that little car, exposing her nyloned legs, and talking about college and music. I remember hearing the Carpenters sing "Close To You" on the radio, and Terri singing along. Man, she looked hot, while gazing out the window of my VW bug.

When we got to the Santa Monica Aud, it was already dark. But the parking lot was replete with the popular motor vehicles of the time: Customized vans with rims and psychedelic paint jobs; VW's, like mine, with scoops and fog lights; Mach Ones and Dusters and wide-wheeled Chevys, driven by the low-riders with organ pipes in the back and fancy script on the windows. Most of these automotive sobriquets were the titles of popular songs, like "Crystal Blue Persuasion,"" Na Na Hey Hey Kiss Him Goodbye" or "Mama Told Me Not To Come."

Driving these "extensions of one's personality," along with the pompadoured low-riders, were the "long hairs"— the dudes with hair down past their shoulders. They were the second wave of hippies who were basically repulsed by the flowers, beads, incense and "make love not war" slogans of the Haight Ashbury crowd. These "long hairs" were the "Woodstock aficionados"— pot smokers with a hard core edge to them. Their slogans were "Fuck Nixon," "Fuck The Pig" "Fuck Vietnam" and "Fuck The Government." They surfed, cruised, worked, attended junior college and balled anything that walked on two female legs.

MIND TAVERN

I remember vividly as Terri and I walked into the auditorium the distant but extremely loud sound of Savoy Brown, the other group in concert, blasting out their "Savoy Brown Boogie." It was very ear numbing to say the least, but the guitar playing of Kim Simmonds was great. They must've played the "Boogie" non-stop for at least an hour, all the while, everyone was standing on their chairs, smoking pot as it was passed to them, and dancing the night away.

While all this was going on, this freak with purple lips and reeking of clove cigarettes approached us and handed me a tiny green slip of paper advertising a "Kiss In," a big Labor Day rock festival in Venice with the Bongo Kings, whoever they were. I remember laughing at the little green slip of paper with X'x all over it and saying to Terri: "These freaks want another Woodstock, but a much nastier one than last year's festival."

I heard later that the "Kiss In" was busted by the cops, and that the promoters were a bunch of Satanists, who were bent on the ruination of as many young souls as possible.

Anyway, Terri and I rocked out for two or three hours, listening to Savoy Brown and the great Johnny Winter. That guy was a true freak; an albino long hair who reminded me of a ghost as he slid around on stage with his new band, "And." Both Terri and I thought Rick Derringer was just as hot a guitarist as Winter; maybe not as fast, but he definitely knew his licks. Personally I was disappointed because Winter didn't play "Fast Life Rider" or "Memory Pain" from his Second Winter album. He mostly played new stuff that would eventually appear on his third album with his new band. Nevertheless, the concert was a great experience. I never saw so many hot hippie chicks in one place before.

A Young Hippie Learns About Classical Music

The best class I had the pleasure of taking while a student at Rio Hondo College during the Fall of 1970 was "Music Appreciation 101" The professor was this bespectacled lady named Dr. Wells, and I credit her alone for turning me on to "classical" music. Initially I thought this particular class was a big bore. Terri R, the object of my libido at the time, was my classmate, and frankly, all I really wanted to do during the class hour was stare at her shiny smooth legs and bulging breasts from beneath her tight sweaters. Needless to say, I was not altogether interested in listening to some ancient lady go on and on about Bach, Mozart and Sonata Form.

But everything changed when I heard Debussy's "Prelude To The Afternoon Of A Faun" for the first time. The shimmering sounds of the orchestra, especially the harp and flute, sent chills down my spine, and I became transfixed. It was like a revelation to me at the time. This was real romantic music; music I could play on my parents' living room stereo with the fireplace aglow; music with which I could romance a chick, and maybe, just maybe, I might be able to 'cop a feel' in the process. From that point on, my interest in classical music was like a tidal wave.

Next came the Etudes of Chopin. I had never heard such emotionally charged music like this before. The Etude in E major, opus 10 number 3, stands out in my mind as one of the best pieces of all piano literature. His music, in my opinion, epitomizes all that is "romantic."

Ludwig van Beethoven is another favorite composer who had a major impact upon my young mind. His 5th piano concerto, "The Emperor," especially the "Adagio un poco mosso," is music only a god could have written. I remember playing that work of art continuously during the spring of 1971. I was a 19 year old maniac with a bushy beard and rampaging hormones. This was perfect make-out music.

Eventually, my interest in Beethoven blossomed and I bought a Leonard Bernstein album that included the 5th and 9th symphonies. Again, I was awestruck by the power and sheer genius of Beethoven's orchestration. When I played his "Ode To Joy" movement from the 9th, I considered it the next best thing to having a McDonald's cheeseburger. I can remember during a stifling heat wave in Southern California, I painted my parents' house to the incessant rhythms of the 9th. I still vividly recall dipping my paint brush into a beige paint can, all the while, whistling the vibrant harmonies of what I consider to be the greatest of all the symphonies.

Mozart was also a major turn-on for me during my college days. I learned what Sonata Form is by analyzing his 40th symphony. One of my all-time favorite classical pieces is his Flute and Harp Concerto in C Minor. I have been inspired to write many poems, both good and bad, while listening to this stunning piece of music.

George Gershwin's Rhapsody In Blue and the Piano Concerto in F are two works I can recall playing to death from 1971 until 1972. Gershwin's urbanesque style on the piano appealed to my 19 year old psyche, especially his Preludes. They are little miniature gems of pure Jazz. All his piano work is highly recommended.

Aaron Copland's "Appalachian Spring" is one piece I played whenever I became depressed over breakups with my various girlfriends. Thanks to the Leonard Bernstein recording on Columbia, and Copland himself, I didn't commit suicide at age 21 over those traumatic breakups.

Gustav Mahler became an intense obsession of mine during the spring of 1973. His "Resurrection" and 9th Symphonies are, frankly, two mind rushes that have to be experienced in the darkness of a small room, late at night with headphones and a glass of chablis. The 9th literally dies. It is definitely one of the most profound musical pieces I have ever heard. His 8th symphony is another mind blower. The last 20 minutes of this symphony is one of my all time favorite musical moments. Exhilarating and profound, this piece literally raptures you away into the farthest corners of the cosmos. Listening to it loud is a must.

French Impressionist, Erik Satie, has to be my all-time favorite composer. Dennis F turned me on to this absurdist genius's music in 1974, when he procured the Vox Box compilation, performed by Frank Glazer. Every piece by him conjures up in my mind memories of countless past days and nights, of kicking back in my Hoover Street den and listening to this unique piano music. I might add that his "Nocturnes" and "Sports Et divertissements" are the perfect musical accompaniments for a lazy afternoon in bed with your lover. They are to be played low, perhaps even better at night, with a single candle flickering. Satie is indeed my chief musical obsession—one that has lasted continuously since 1974.

INDEX

A
Air; Playground Love 58
Alan Parsons Project; Can't Take It With You 34
Allman Brothers Band; Jessica 6, You Don't Love Me 15
Animals; Monterey 105
Anka, Paul; Diana 87
Aphex Twin; We Are The Music Makers 75

B
Bach, J.S.; Toccata and Fugue in D Minor 94
Barber, Samuel; Excursions for Piano, Op. 20 72
Barroso, Ary and Gilbert, Ray; Baia 77
Bartok, Bela; String Quartet #2 103, Piano Concerto #3 109
Beach Boys; 409 134, Good Vibrations 138
Beethoven, Ludwig Van; Moonlight Sonata 67, Symphony #9 72
Belafonte, Harry; Cocoanut Woman 89
Bernstein, Leonard; *On the Town* 69-70, Fancy Free Ballet 69, Prelude, Fugue and Riffs for Solo Clarinet 70
Berry, Chuck; School Days 2, Sweet Little Sixteen 6
Big Bopper; Big Bopper's Wedding 86
Bizet, Georges; L'Arlesienne Suite" #1 110
Blind Faith; Presence of the Lord 52
Blood Sweat and Tears; And When I Die 104, *Blood, Sweat & Tears* 148
Bloomfield, Mike and Kooper, Al; I Wonder Who 75
Bolcom, William; War in Heaven 94
Bonds, Gary "U.S."; New Orleans 133

Borodin, Alexander; Dances of the Polovtsi 108, Nocturne Promenade 108
Brahms, Johannes; Intermezzo for Piano 28, Piano Concerto #1 in D Minor 59
Buffalo Springfield; Bluebird 2, Pretty Girl Why 109, Special Care 109, Uno Mundo 109

C

Cactus; Parchman Farm 5
Canned Heat; Dust My Broom 31, Woodstock Boogie 108
Cash, Johnny; *At Folsom Prison* 150
Chabrier, Emmanuel; Dix Pieces Pittoresques 65
Channel, Bruce; Hey! Baby 134
Charles, Ray; Ruby 57, You Don't Know Me 57
Chiffons; He's So Fine 135
Chopin, Frederick; Polonaise Fantaisie 67, Etude in E 68
Chordettes; Mr. Sandman 87
Cline, Patsy ; Crazy, Walkin' After Midnight 39
Cocker, Joe; With a Little Help From My Friends 14, Delta Lady 100, Feelin' Alright 100
Cole, Nat "King"; Mona Lisa 57, Too Young 57
Coltrane, John; Moment's Notice 47
Copland, Aaron; Appalachian Spring 64, 73 160, Billy the Kid 70
Count Basie; Lester Leaps In 9
Cream; Crossroads 3, Stepping Out 15, Traintime 27, Deserted Cities of the Heart 51
Creedence Clearwater Revival; Ramble Tamble 4
Crosby Stills Nash and Young; Woodstock 52

D

Dave Brubeck Quartet; Blue Rondo a La Turk 44, Take Five 44, 47
Davis, Miles; All Blues 46, 48, Flamenco Sketches 48, *Bitches Brew* 146
Dead Can Dance; Mother Tongue 27
Debussy, Claude; Rhapsody for Orchestra and Alto Saxophone 8, "Sirenes" from *Nocturnes* 8, Danses Sacree Et Profane 32, Des pas sur la Neige 66, Reverie 95
Deep Purple; Smoke On The Water 76
Dell Vikings; Come Go With Me 84

Denisov, Edison; Sonata for Alto Saxophone and Piano 10
Derrick and the Dominoes; *Layla and other assorted love songs* 146
Di Lasso, Orlando; Timor Et Tremor 9
Dick Dale and the Del-Tones; King of the Surf Guitar 2, Hava Nagila 2
Dickens, "Little" Jimmy; May the Bird of Paradise Fly Up Your Nose 39
Dorsey, Jimmy; So Rare 27
Dream Theater; The Root of All Evil 58
Dylan, Bob; Pledging My Time 56, Most Likely You Go Your Way And I'll Go Mine 56, Oxford Town 136, Subterranean Homesick Blues 137, *Bringing It All Back Home* 151

E
El Mariachi Aquila De Guadalajara; La Vaquilla 34
Emerson Lake and Palmer; *Pictures at an Exhibition* 16
Eno, Brian; Lizard Point 79, Lantern Marsh 79, Unfamiliar Wind 79, M386 80, Failing Light 80, Late October 80, Lost in the Humming Air 80, 2/1 80, Ikebukuro 81, Evening Star 81, An Index of Metals 81
Everly Brothers; Wake Up Little Susie 88, Walk Right Back 134

F
Fats Waller and His Rhythm; I'm Crazy 'Bout My Baby 30
Field, John; Nocturnes 27
Fitzgerald, Ella; How High the Moon 46
Foghat; Slow Ride 6
Fontaine, Eddie; Nothin' Shakin' 86
Fotine, Larry; Fascination Rag 33
Fripp, Robert; Under Heavy Manners 35

G
Gabriel, Peter; The Family and the Fishing Net 26, Here Comes the Flood 62, Darkness 62
Gaye, Marvin; *What's Going On* 153
Genesis; The Knife 94
Gentle Giant; Peel the Paint 58, *Interview* 94, 111, Octopus 101, Design 111
Gershwin, George; Oh Lady Be Good 34, Rhapsody in Blue 63, 70, 71, 160, Piano Concerto in F 70, 160

Grand Funk Railroad; Inside Looking Out 4, In Need 50
Grateful Dead; China Cat Sunflower 17
Gregorian Chant; Christe Redemptor 7
Grieg, Edvard; Wedding Day At Troldhaugen 68

H
Havens, Richie; Handsome Johnny 99
Haydn, Franz Joseph; Concerto in E Flat for Trumpet 40
Holtz, Gustav; Neptune, *The Planets* 10
Hunter, Tab; Young Love 86

I
Ibert, Jacques; Concertino for Alto Saxophone and Eleven Instruments 9
Iron Butterfly; In-A-Gadda-Da-Vida 139

J
Jackson, Michael; The Way You Make Me Feel 104
Janis Joplin and Big Brother & The Holding Company; Ball and Chain 98
Jethro Tull; Inside 111
Jimi Hendrix Experience; Voodoo Chile Live Version 2, 1983…(A Merman I Should Turn To Be) 28, Who Knows 100, Exp 128, Up From the Skies 128, If 6 Was 9 129, You Got Me Floatin' 129, Little Miss Lover 129, And the Gods Made Love 129, Come On (Part 1) 130, Voodoo Child (Slight Return) 130
John Lee Hooker and Canned Heat; Whiskey and Wimmen 109
John, Elton; *Goodbye Yellow Brick Road* 149

K
King Crimson; Prince Rupert's Lament 4, Formentera Lady 11, B'Boom 26, Starless and Bible Black 29, Dangerous Curves 61, Lark's Tongues in Aspic 61
Kingston Trio; Tom Dooley 88
Kraftwerk; Autobahn 62, The Model 62

L
Lanza, Mario; Be My Love 31
Led Zeppelin; The Rover 6, Bring It On Home 52, Dazed and Confused 139
Lee, Brenda; I'm Sorry 133
Lennon, John; Found Out 5,

Cold Turkey 16, Yer Blues 99, Don't Worry Kyoto (Mummy's Only Looking For Her Hand In The Snow) 99, *Imagine 152,*
Lennox, Annie; Don't Let It Bring You Down 76
Ligeti, Gyorgy; Magany 10, Ket Kanor 10
Little Richard; Keep A Knockin 85

M

Mahler, Gustav; Songs of a Wayfarer 30, Symphony No. 2 40, Symphony #8 72
Massenet, Jules; Meditation from 'Thais 111
Mayall, John; Room to Move 16, Exercise in C Major for Harmonica, Bass and Shufflers 32
Mayall, John, and the Bluesbreakers; *Bluesbreakers with Eric Clapton* 152
Mendelssohn, Felix; Sonata for Piano, Op 6 76
Midnight Oil; Only the Strong 26
Milhaud, Darius; Scaramouche, Suite for Alto Saxophone and Orchestra 8
Modern Jazz Quartet; The Devil and the Deep Blue Sea 44, Night in Tunisia 48, Delauney's Delimma 70

Monk, Thelonious; Bye-Ya 45
Montez, Chris; Let's Dance 134
Moody Blues; Legend of a Mind 32, Never Thought I'd Live To Be A Hundred 50, Leave This Man Alone 122, Voices in the Sky 123, Never Comes the Day 123, It's Up To You 124, Procession 124, You and Me 125
Morrison, Van; *Astral Weeks* 149
Mountain; Stormy Monday 14

N

Nelson, Ricky; I'm Walkin 84
Nirvana; In Bloom 6, The Man Who Sold the World 104

P

Part, Arvo; Summa for Strings 29
Partch, Harry; Castor and Pollux 63
Pink Floyd; *The Dark Side of the Moon* 145
Pook, Jocelyn; Migrations 25
Porcupine Tree; Dead Wing 58
Presley, Elvis; Teddy Bear 86, Hound Dog 88, 98
Prima, Louis and Smith, Keely; That Old Black Magic 47
Procol Harum; *Broken Barricades 150*
Prokofiev, Serge; Lt. Kije Suite 59

Q
Quicksilver Messenger Service; Mona 14

R
Rachmaninov, Sergei; Vespers 9, Prelude in C Sharp Minor 68
Rage Against The Machine; Killing in the Name 93
Rainwater, Marvin; So You Think You Got Troubles 84
Ravel, Maurice; Oiseaux Tristes 66, La Vallee des Cloches 66
Ray, Johnny; Street of Memories 87

RENIERS, WENDY LIST:
  Eddie Fisher; Oh Cindy 92
  Jim Lowe; Green Door 92
  Patience and Prudence; Tonight You Belong To Me 92
  Perry Como; Hot Diggity 92
  Teresa Brewer; A Sweet Old Fashioned Girl 92
  Al Hibbler; He 92
  Randy Starr; After School 92
  Jimmy Bowen; Warm Up To Me Baby 92
  Buddy Knox; Party Doll 92
  Pat Boone; Why Baby Why 92
  Ricky Nelson; A Teenager's Romance 92
  Ferlin Husky; Gone 92
  Jill Corey; Love Me To Pieces 92
  Bruce Adams; Knee Deep in the Blues 92
  Gale Storm; Dark Moon 92
  Billy Williams; Date With The Blues 92
  Dottie Evans; Lucky Lips 93
  Jack Daniels; Somebody Up There Likes Me 93
  Janice Harper; Bon Voyage 93
  Andy Williams; Lips of Wine 93
  Paul Anka; Tell Me That You Love Me 93
  Jimmy Bowen; Cross Over 93
  Louis Nye; Hi-Ho Steve-O 93
  Billy Williams Got a Date with an Angel 93
  Carol Jarvis; Rebel 93

Riley, Terry; In C 95
Robbins, Marty; El Paso 37, A White Sport Coat 84
Rodrigo, Joaquin; Adagio 110, Concierto de Aranjuez for Guitar and Orchestra 110
Rolling Stones; Midnight Rambler – Live 76, Paint It Black 98, Doncha Bother Me 118, Flight 505 118, It's Not Easy 118, Cool,

Calm & Collected 118, Miss Amanda Jones 119, Parachute Woman 119, Prodigal Son 119, Dead Flowers 119, Sister Morphine 119, Pass The Wine 119, Turd On The Run 120
Royal Teens; Planet Rock 85

S
Saint-Saens, Camille; Le Deluge Op. 45 73
Sands, Jodie; With All My Heart 85
Sartori and Quarantotto; Con Te Partiro, sung by Andrea Bocelli 76
Satie, Erik; Nocturnes 72, 160
Savoy Brown; Savoy Brown Boogie 4, 53, 158
Schubert, Franz; Ave Maria 11
Seville, David; Gotta Get To Your House 84, The Chipmunk Song 88
Shankar, Ravi; Raga Bhimpatasi 59
Sibelius, Jean; Valse Triste 33
Sinatra, Frank; In the Wee Small Hours of the Morning 46
Smith, Jimmy; Come On Baby 45
Sonny and Cher; I Got You Babe 137
South, Joe; The Purple People Eater Meets The Witch Doctor 87
Spacemen 3; Come Down Easy 105, Transparent Radiation 106
Springsteen, Bruce; *Born to Run* 150
Steely Dan; *Aja* 148
Stephen Lee; Blood Was Its Avatar 5
Stravinsky, Igor; Petrushka for Orchestra 41, Petrushka for Piano 41, The Rite of Spring 113-114

SULLLIVAN, ED SHOW VIDEO LIST
Elvis Presley; Hound Dog 98
Buddy Holly and the Crickets; Peggy Sue 98
Beatles; I Want To Hold Your Hand 98
Beach Boys; I Get Around 98
Animals; Don't Bring Me Down 98
The Doors; Light My Fire 98
Steppenwolf; Born To Be Wild 98
Chambers Brothers; Time Has Come Today 98
Creedence Clearwater Revival; Proud Mary 98
Sly and the Family Stone; Dance To The Music 98
Martha and the Vandellas; Dancing In The Streets 98

T

Tatum, Art; Somebody Loves Me 45, Plaid 75

Tchaikovsky, Peter; Berceuse, from *18 Piano Pieces* 66, Violin Concerto in D 71, Symphony #6 72,

Ten Years After; I'm Going Home 3

The Band; We Can Talk 53

The Beatles; *Abbey Road* 19, Get Back 51, Do You Want To Know A Secret 135, I'm Happy Just To Dance With You 136, Paperback Writer 138

The Browns; The Three Bells 38

The Byrds; Eight Miles High 17, *Younger Than Yesterday* 147

The Clash; *London Calling* **145**

The Doors; Celebration of the Lizard 17, The End 138

The Keith Jarret Trio; Butch and Butch 62

The Kingsmen; Louie, Louie 11

The Kinks; All Day and All of the Night 137

The Marcels; Blue Moon 133

The Miracles; Going To A Go-Go 138

The Mothers of Invention; Trouble Every Day 77

The Playmates; Beep Beep 85

The Who; Magic Bus 100, My Generation 100, Magic Bus -Live 15

This Mortal Coi; Drugs 26

Traffic; *Traffic* 149

W

Waits, Tom; Step Right Up 57

Walker, Charlie; Pick Me Up On Your Way Down 38

War; Spill the Wine 93

Weissenberg, Alexis; Pianist for Petrushka 1965 41

Welch, Lenny; Since I Fell For You 135

Williams, Billy; I'm Gonna Sit Right Down and Write Myself a Letter 89

Williams, Hank; Why Don't You Love Me 105, *Mercury Recordings 1947-1952* 152

Williams, Vaughn; Romanza from Tuba Concerto in F Minor 71, The Lark Ascending 77

Winter, Johnny; Hustled Down in Texas 3, Fast Life Rider 10, 158 Memory Pain 51, 158, Tribute To Muddy 110

Y

Yes; Leave It 105

Young, Neil; *Live Rust 151*

YOUTUBE LIST:
Johnny Crawford; When the Folks High Up Do The Mean Low-Down 141
Jean Luc Ponty; Individual Choice 142
Animusic.com; Pipe Dream 142
Vaughn Williams; Tuba Concerto, Romanza 142
Jeff Buckley; Dream Brother 142
Brice Salek; Avant- Garde Electronic Music Meditations 142
Sonya, the Belly Dancer 143
Braindrop; Avant-Garde Symphony and Frequency Shifter 143
Francis Poulenc; Trois Novelettes 143
Terry Riley; A Rainbow in Curved Air 143
Erik Satie; La Diva de l'Empire 144
Frank Sinatra; One For My Baby (and one more for the road) 144

Z
Zappa, Frank; Willie the Pimp 4
Zombies; *Odessey and Oracle* 147

ABOUT THE AUTHOR

BORN IN WHITTIER, CALIFORNIA in 1952, Stark Hunter was an English teacher for 38 years before retiring from the classroom in 2017. He has written and published 13 books, which are available on Amazon.com and Barnes & Noble.com: *In A Gadda Da Vida*, a novel, published in 2002, *Carnivorous Avenues*, a poetry volume published in 2004, *Flies*, a short novel published in 2005, *Private Diaries*, a satire published in 2006, *Voices From Clark Cemetery*, a poetry volume published in 2013, *Cocktails For the Soul*, a poetry anthology published in 2013, *Voices From Mt. Olive Cemetery*, a poetry volume published in 2018, *Digested by the Dust*, another poetry anthology, published in 2018, *Scenes From the Cerebellum*, published in 2019, *Monster Trees*, published in 2020, *White Sidewalks* in 2021, *Covid Gardens*, anti-poetry published in 2021, and *The Pink Oleanders* in 2022.

Hunter's work has also been published by the following literary journals: Lothlorien Poetry Journal, SpillWords Press, Synchronized Chaos, Silent Spark Press, and the Hong Kong Review.

His poetry was included in the several Poetry Anthologies, including: *Stars In Our Hearts, Visions*, published 2012 (World Poetry Movement); *In My Lifetime, Chronicles*, published 2013 (Eber and Wein Publishing); *PS: It's Poetry, An Anthology Of Eclectic Contemporary Poems Written By Poets From Around the Globe*, published 2020 (PoetrySoup.Com).

Fourteen of Mr. Hunter's poems from *Voices From Clark Cemetery* were adopted and set to music by Dr. George Mabry, composer and former conductor of the Nashville Symphony Chorus, for his work, *Voices*, a musical drama which was performed at Austin Peay State University in Clarksville, Tennessee in 2015.

Mr. Hunter's poetry works can be perused at poetrysoup.com. and allpoetry.com.

Stark Hunter is also the creator and producer of over 200 musical works, all published at SoundCloud.com, a free music streaming platform with an audience of 76 million listeners.

Mr. Hunter is married with two daughters, a granddaughter and a grandson, and resides in Chino Hills, California.

www.ingramcontent.com/pod-product-compliance
Lightning Source LLC
Chambersburg PA
CBHW030856170426

43193CB00009BA/625